DAY TRADING FOR BEGINNERS GUIDE:

THE BEST STOCK MARKET STRATEGIES TO CREATE PASSIVE INCOME FOR A LIVING, HOW TO MAKE MONEY WITH OPTIONS, FOREX AND SWING TRADE TO REACH THE FINANCIAL FREEDOM.

BRANDON BLUEPRINTS

DISCLAIMER

Table Of Contents

Description

Successful day trading is a journey; it's not a destination. In this journey, you're going to change. In this journey, you're going to be challenged. Your level of discipline, self-control, and your ability to look at the big picture over a long period of time are going to be tested. Accordingly, you need to look at the tools and tactics that I've mentioned in this book to help you get a proper context for day trading. Ultimately, it's your mindset that will determine if you'll be a successful day trader or not.

While it's easy to look at day trading success as a simple matter of failing or succeeding, it's not that simple. The vast majority of day traders are actually in the middle. They haven't completely failed, but they haven't succeeded either. They're just treading water; they're settling on cents on the dollar.

This is too bad because by simply adopting the right psychology, which leads to increased level of discipline, you'll be able to have a broad view of day trading. This broad view would enable you to scale up properly and employ the right tactics so you can go from simply being lucky from time to time to consistently getting the results that you came for.

As with doing anything, you need to have the passion for trading to be a great trader. You have to find joy in what you do on a daily basis. With day trading, you can find happiness in one day and despair in the next if you are not careful. When the going gets tough and you are going through a bad streak, you will definitely question yourself about doing day trading and whether it has been the right decision. A sane person will give up to cut their losses; a passionate person will get to the bottom of why he is failing and come back an even better trader. He will play to his strengths and learn from his mistakes; he will not be emotional when he screws up because he knows that losing is part of the game. He will remain focused on the ultimate goal, which is to be consistent in the market. He will be happy at the end of the day whether it's a red or green day because he has learnt something from the day and more importantly, he enjoyed the process.

This guide will focus on the following:

- Day trading basics

- Basics of performing a trade

- Types of day trading

- Building a watchlist

- Trading and time

- Finding the top day trading picks

- Techniques to employ in day trading

- Developing your target price

- The autotrading function explained

- Intraday candlestick pattern

- Bollinger band bounce trading strategy

- First hour trading

- Momentum

- Things you should not do while day trading

- Trading and commitment

- Exit Strategies

- The secrets of successful day traders... AND MORE!!!

Introduction

Day trading is quite different and difficult from other trading styles, due to the short time frame for making decisions related to entry and exit points.

The basic investing rule for intraday trading is don't trust what you think, trust what you see. Understanding the basics of day trading and experiment with those basics with the help of demo accounts could help intraday traders to make big gains. Intraday trading also involves several trading strategies and indicators to maximize returns and reduce losses. If you don't have a strong command on the technical side, the risk of losing the trade is higher.

Although risking 1% may not appear like a ton to hazard in any trade, and this allows investors to generate better returns even if their losing trader are higher than winning trades. When the day trader just risks 1%, he should expect to generate 1.5% to 3% profit target on each trade. For instance, the day trader is risking $150 to make $200 to $300 looks like a good strategy to generate better overall returns.

The markets never move in a straight line nor are they always consolidating and trending. Day traders also have to manage distinctive kinds of unpredictability and uncertainties. Therefore, day traders should also know how to trade in a volatile environment, and they should also understand how they can use different indicators to manage the volatility.

Day traders should always know about different trends, breakouts, and sideways trading if they want to succeed in day trading. Analyzing charts and predicting trends could become easier for day traders if they do some training before trading with real cash.

The volume indicators are significantly important in stock picking and making entry and exit points. If you understand the volumes, it is among the easiest way of deciding on the selling and buying activity of any stock at important levels. However, the complicated element is that volumes can offer contradictory signals for a similar system. Nevertheless, a trader's potential to evaluate what actually the volume movement is signaling in combination with stock price movement could be among the deciding factors for profit-making potential.

Day traders are suggested to wait for the stock price to reach close to the high of the range and afterward turn back lower. This will give an okay signal, and the exchange is left at, or close to, the low of the range. You may need to rehash the way toward purchasing at the support level and offering at protection commonly until the point when the stock breaks out of the channel!

Chapter 1- Day Trading Basics

Margin Accounts and Leverage

Once you've picked your brokerage, you'll need to decide what type of account you will create. Usually as a day trader you will be using a "margin account". This can be distinguished from a "cash account", where your buying power would be limited to the capital you provide and nothing more. While it's certainly possible to make money by trading with just cash, margin trading is the big reason why day trading can be so lucrative.

When you use a margin account, your brokerage will loan you money to buy assets in addition to the capital you provide. The stock, or other assets, you buy will be collateral for the loan. This loan, trading "on margin" allows you to "leverage" your buying power - so any profits you make will be bigger, since you can buy more shares than you could with cash. Of course, trading on margin also increases your risk. So if you don't have a good trading plan or strategy, your losses trading on margin can also be bigger than if you trade with cash. If you lose too much money, your broker may require you to pay back the loan with your own capital.

The amount of leverage you use can vary. Most day traders who invest in stocks use a leverage ratio of 4:1. This gives you 4 times the buying power with the potential to make 4 times the profit. Depending on your broker or your available capital, you may be limited to a 2:1 ratio. In some markets, you can trade with even more leverage - some day traders on the FOREX exchange will trade with 50:1 leverage.

Taking Advantage of the Big Traders

These days, most trading in the market is done by big firms who engage in high-volume trading ("HVT"). HVT is the practice of trading very large numbers of shares in very short periods of time, with the trades being picked by powerful super-computers running complex algorithms.

Some critics have argued that HVT is bad for the market, and that the calculations performed by investment computers have gotten so complex that nobody, not even the programmers, understand them anymore. HVT may have been what caused the "flash crash" in 2010, an incident where the value of the DOW fell nearly 1,600 points in 36 minutes. Analysts theorize that HVT algorithms were reacting to the actions of other HVT trades in a cascade that ran out of control. While there hasn't been another incident as bad as the original flash crash, similar falls have occurred on a semi-regular basis since then.

While there may be negative aspects to the dominance of the modern market by big HVT traders, these big traders also create opportunities for day traders to make it big themselves. Big investment firms add lots of volatility and volume to the market by making millions of trades a day on the tiniest changes in price, market conditions, and breaking news. This means that prices move up and down a lot more from minute to minute than they did when traders had to meet face to face.

With careful planning and a well thought out strategy, you can take advantage of these swings in price to make money as a day trader.

Writing a Trading Plan

Before you do anything else with your brokerage account, you should write a trading plan. Your trading plan is a written document that details your chosen trading strategy, sets profit goals, and defines your parameters for risk-management. This could be your perfect long-term plan that you stick with for your entire career as a day trader, or it could be an ever-changing document that adjusts to your situation and the market. Many day traders will write a trading plan every single session, so their strategy matches current market conditions.

If you don't have a trading plan, you're basically just gambling. A plan prevents you from acting impulsively and limits your risk to what you can handle. You should consider your level of experience, your current mental state, and the news of the day. After you have more experience, you may consider writing your plans in a way that better matches your personal style. However, until then, your plan should always contain: your risk management rules, your trading strategy, your entry rules, and your exit rules.

Risk Management: the first step in any good trading plan is setting your rules for risk management. This includes limits on how much risk to take on any single trade as well as overall limits on acceptable losses (daily stop-loss). Most day traders will not risk more than 1% of their total capital on any given trade - setting a limit like this is an important tool to limit your exposure. Your plan should also contain your daily stop loss - an amount of losses where you exit the market for the day.

Strategy: the next step in making your trading plan is to pick what strategy you will be using for the day. Your strategy is how you pick stocks and identify potential trades. Consider your mood and whether you're well rested. Do you want to be an active trader all day, or just pull off a couple low risk trades early? How is the market trending - is it up, or down, or flat? Is there any breaking news? All of these factors can inform what strategy is appropriate for that day. It's even possible that you may want to simply sit back and observe for an entire session - just watching charts can increase your ability to read trends and make more money later.

Entry Rules: after you've picked your strategy, set your entry rules. This is the set of conditions you are looking for before entering a trade. Be thorough - what types of pattern are you looking for, how many different circumstances need to line up, how much profit potential is there in the trend you're watching?

Exit Rules: your exit rules have two elements: your price target and your stop-loss. Your price-target is the point you will exit the market after making the desired profit. The stop-loss is the point where you plan to exit when you've made a bad bet.

What Time of Day to Trade?

Maybe you're looking to start day trading full time. Or maybe you're looking to trade a little bit on the side. While an all-day trading session can provide more opportunities, it's not necessarily more lucrative. There's a few reasons for this. First, day trading is a very intense and draining activity - the longer you go in a single session, the less effective you are likely to be. Second, most of your best opportunities to make big trades will occur in the hours immediately after the market opens and immediately before the market closes.

A common piece of advice for new traders is to not take any trades in the first 15 minutes after the opening bell. These early minutes are the most volatile and least predictable time of day, so it's a good time to keep an eye out for developing trends and to get a feeling for the mood of the market by watching the major indexes. Most traders recommend trading during the active hours that follow - roughly from 8:30 AM to 11:30 AM Eastern Standard Time.

If you're also looking to capitalize on late market movement, you can add a fourth hour of trading immediately before the closing bell, from 3:00 PM to 4:00 PM Eastern Standard Time. Like the opening period, this is also a time with high volatility and profit potential.

Start slow, only trading two or three hours a day. Figure out what works for you. If you feel like you can go longer, experiment with that as well. Just keep in mind that working longer isn't necessarily more profitable - your priority should always be on making the best trades, not the most trades.

Mechanics of Trading

Now that you know about how to write a trading plan and have some idea of what hours you should be getting into the market, we're ready for an overview of the actual mechanics of executing day trades.

Market Orders: your primary means of interacting with the market is through market orders. A market order is a request for your broker to facilitate the purchase or sale of an asset. By default, your broker will find the best available price as soon as possible.

Limit Order: a limit order is a special type of market order that places conditions on the purchase or sale of the target asset. Most of your trades will be made using limit orders. Generally, when you place a limit order, you ask your broker to purchase or sell the target asset for a price within a limited range. You will be using limit orders to set your entry points, profit targets, and stop-losses.

Price Target: your price target is the price you are planning to sell the target asset at. How much profit you are looking to extract on a transaction will depend on your chosen strategy: a scalping strategy sets the price target at a point barely above commission, while a momentum strategy may set the price target much higher. In most cases, you will set a limit order to automatically sell the target asset when it reaches the price target defined by your strategy.

Stop-Loss: your stop-loss is the point where it's become clear that you've made a losing bet and it's time to limit your exposure. You should always set a stop-loss order on a trade, for example 10% below your purchase price, so when things go bad you get out before they get worse.

Daily Stop-loss: besides placing limit orders to define stop-loss on individual trades, you should also have a daily stop-loss set. Many traders will set their daily stop-loss at 3% of total capital. If you've lost on multiple trades and are down by 3% for the day, you're probably upset, frustrated, and not thinking clearly. Continuing to trade under these conditions will probably put you even deeper in the hole.

Daily Profit Target: you should also set a daily profit goal. While it may be tempting to continue trading after you've made your daily profit target, doing so risks over-confidence and excessively risky trades. In most cases, it's best to quit while you're ahead.

Active Trading: beyond setting limit orders, you may also choose to be an active trader. When you are actively trading, you will monitor the performance of your ongoing trades and adjust the parameters of your limits to increase your profits where appropriate.

Assessing your performance - Win-rate and profit / loss: at the end of every trading day and trading week you should assess your performance to make sure you are maintaining profitability. There are two primary measures of performance for trading strategies: win-rate and profit / loss ratio (P/L).

Your win-rate is the percentage of transactions that are profitable. Your P/L is calculated by dividing the average profit on winning trades over the average loss on losing trades across the relevant time-period. In general, to be profitable, you should have a win-rate of at least 50% and a P/L of at least 1.25. If either are lower, it may be time to consider changing your strategy.

Tax Considerations for Day Trading

You may be wondering about how the money you will make as a day trader will be taxed. This can get pretty complex, so we won't cover it in detail in this book. If you want to make sure you are handling your taxes on income from day trading correctly, we strongly recommend that you get an accountant. However, we'll cover some of the basics here:

Capital Gains and Losses: making money as a trader isn't like getting paid wages. Income from trading securities is classified as "capital gains" by the Internal Revenue Service (IRS). If you've never had capital gains before, you should be prepared for your tax preparation to be more complicated than you're used to. Fortunately, your broker will provide a summary document called a 1099-B that covers all the details - all you need to report the IRS are the top-line numbers. Here's a quick run-down of how this works:

When you make a profit on a trade, you have taxable "capital gains" income from that transaction. The gain is the difference between your purchase and sale price. When you lose on a trade, you are considered to have a "capital loss". If you end a year with a net capital loss, you may be able to use that loss to offset other income in that year or other years.

Things You Should Never Do While Day Trading

We'll finish off this chapter with a big list of the thirteen things you should never do while day trading. If any of this seems repetitive, that's just because some of these points - like managing risk - are really important. Keep these things in mind before you make a big mistake.

(1) Never trade without a plan: if this wasn't clear already, let's make it clear now. You should never day trade without a well thought out trading plan defining your trading strategy, risk management, and goals.

(2) Never trade with unrealistic expectations: don't plan to get rich overnight. Maybe you'll get lucky, but it's much more likely that you won't. The trick to making money is to be patient, with small, achievable goals - if you keep your expectations realistic, you won't reach for the sun and get burned.

(3) Never trade with too much leverage: we've talked a lot about how important margin trading is to bigger

profits. Never forget that margin trading cuts both ways - bigger rewards require bigger risks. If you're trading in an extremely leveraged position, such as the 50:1 ratio used by some FOREX traders, a tiny loss of 1% has the potential to wipe out your entire capital position.

(4) Never trade too frequently: be patient! Don't be too tempted to jump on mediocre trades - you won't make as much money off them, and they aren't worth the risk. Instead, wait for the good set-ups identified by your trading strategy and your trading plan.

(5) Never trade without doing the homework first: don't jump into a trade just because you've seen a pattern on the charts that looks like a promising opportunity. Do the work: analyze the charts, check the trends, research the company and the news (if your strategy calls for it). After you've gotten some experience, maybe you'll be able to identify a trade at a glance - for now, though, steer clear.

(6) Never stick with a strategy that isn't working for you: not every strategy is going to work for every trader. Keep track of your win-rate and profit / loss ratio. If you aren't maintaining a win rate of at least 50% and a P/L of 1.25, you haven't been making a profit on your chosen

strategy. It may be time to reassess your plan and strategy to figure out what will work for you.

(7) Never trade without setting a stop-loss: always manage your risk. The market can move quickly and unexpectedly. Even the best-looking set-up can be a trap, especially when unexpected news breaks. No trade is a sure thing, so always set a stop-loss according to your trading plan, and you will never get burned too badly.

Chapter 2- Basics of Performing a Trade

Now that you have a good idea of what day trading is and is not, I will go into the basics of performing a trade. This chapter isn't a step-by-step guide to perform your first trade. However, it does describe the main steps you should complete as a day trader. This chapter holds the basic information that you need to know before you arrive to your first day at your new job.

Build Up Your Watchlist

Your watchlist is going to become one of the first things you check in the morning. This list gives you a listing of potential stocks for you on that day. Your watchlist will be made up of dozens of trading tools which will help you make the best decisions possible during your trading day. On top of this, you can continue to observe specific companies to see if you would like to make trades in them at some point. This is a place where you will be able to see patterns within trades and receive up-to-date information about the stock market. Then, once you see that a stock is right where you want it, you can make your next move.

There are thousands of stocks within the market, which means that while you can scan the market as a whole, you will definitely miss a lot if you don't build up the best watchlist as a trader. This watchlist allows you to include the stocks you feel are the best so you can continue to watch them without having to scan the market and go through all the stocks you are not interested in as they never perform well.

Of course, building your watchlist is not as simple as it sounds. However, this doesn't mean that it's impossible or you won't be able to create the best watchlist for your career. It just means that you will need to put in effort, do your homework, and make sure that you understand the environment of the market. Once you reach this point, you will be able to develop the best watchlist for you.

How much effort you have to put into your watchlist will depend on if you are a full-time trader or part-time. If you decide to go the halftime route, you will be able to keep your watchlist simpler. You can get away with having a couple of stocks on your watchlist. However, if you are a committed full-time trader, you will at least want a watchlist that reaches a few more. On top of this, most full-timers will add a second watchlist. This one usually isn't bigger than their main watchlist, but they still put the same amount of effort into their additional list.

Must Have Properties

Before I get into building your watchlist, I want to talk about the three main properties that every watchlist must have.

1. Uniqueness

It is important to make sure that you developed your watchlist to suit your needs. It should have your individual stock market taste that will help you reach the level of success you desire. As a trader, it is important to follow your thoughts, goals, and beliefs. While you will ask for and listen to advice from other traders, you need to make sure you follow your *own* path. In other words, whenever it comes to your detailed plans, like your watchlist, you want to create it. You do not want to rely on anyone else to help you develop your unique list.

2. Repeatability

You want to make sure that whatever detailed plan you create as your watchlist, you are able to complete this every time you sit down to work. Whether you are a part-time or full-time trader, you want it to be consistent and stable so you can repeat your outlined steps every day you trade.

3. Be Realistic

This can become more of an issue for full-time traders than part-time traders. Because part-timers generally have another means of income, they don't always focus heavily on the amount of money their trades bring in. However, full-timers know they have to make a certain amount of money for their budget. Because they usually don't have another way to generate an income, they put more stress on their trades. This can lead to unrealistic expectations within their watchlist. For example, many traders state that it is unrealistic to think you can watch four stocks at one time. Each stock has a large amount of information you need to process, and our minds can only remember so much at a time. Therefore, you are more likely to make mistakes and suffer losses if you are unrealistic with how many stocks you can watch at one time.

You need to make sure that you can manage the workload you place on yourself. Furthermore, the more stressed you become because of your watchlist, the more likely you are to let your emotions start spiking, which can cause you to suffer losses. While you might have to play around with how many stocks you can watch at once, you will want to do this slowly. For example, start with one stock and then work your way up to two. If you find that you can easily manage two stocks, then go up to three. If you find that this is still manageable, but you are unsure if you could handle another stock, then stick with three. You need to stick with what you can manage and what you are comfortable with.

Criteria to Look for When Developing Your Watchlist

Below I will discuss a few guidelines that you should always keep in mind when you are evaluating a stock. These guidelines not only work for when you are thinking of adding a stock to your watchlist but also as you observe the stock from your watchlist.

1. Patterns

It is critical to know the patterns of a stock you are thinking of adding to your watchlist. Through the pattern, you can get a sense of where the stock sits in the market, when a good time to make your move to buy or sell would be, and if the stock is worth your time and effort. The more you watch the pattern of the stock, the easier it is to predict it. However, this doesn't mean that you will be correct every time. In a sense, being wrong here and there is really just a part of the job. But, you want to do what you can to decrease your risk of loss, and one way to do this is by noting the pattern of a stock.

2. Stock analysis

However, I will mention that there are two types of stock analysis. The first type is technical analysis and the second type is fundamental analysis. When you are looking for a stock to add to your watch list, it is important to make note of the stock's analysis. Through the analysis, you will be able to gain the most information about your stock, which is guaranteed to help you make your decision.

3. Amount of risk

You will always want to pay attention to the validity of the stock, which is the amount of risk it holds. You won't want to take on any stocks that are higher than the level of risk you allow yourself in your trading plan. This is especially important for beginners, as you are still learning the basics of trading, so you should *not* take any stocks that are high risk to start with.

What to Avoid in Your Watchlist

Just like there are criteria that you want to pay attention to when adding stocks to your watchlist, there are also things you want to avoid.

1. Do not add dozens of stocks

There are many investors, especially full-time traders, who feel the more stocks they place in their watchlist, the better chance they have of making money. While this might be true for some experienced traders, other top traders state that this is a mistake. In fact, there are many traders such as Timothy Sykes who believe that you want to limit the stocks on your watchlist to a couple and no more than five. For Sykes, it depends on your experience as a trader. If you are just starting out, you will want to stick with one or two. However, if you have several years of experience and find that you can handle a couple more stocks, then you can increase your number.

2. Do not take on large trades

This is another important point if you are new to the trading career. You don't want to take on trades that are too large for you as you will find yourself making mistakes. There is no way that you can win every time as a trader. Therefore, it become more important to keep your trades small. Think of it this way: when you trade small, your loss is going to be small, but if you trade big your loss will also be larger. You want to keep your loss small as you can with any trade, as no matter how much you observe a stock's pattern, you can't predict the future.

Tips for Beginners

However, in order to help you create and manage your first watchlist, here are a few helpful tips.

1. Stay in the now

You want to remember to remain present when you are managing your watchlist. While the historical patterns of a stock can be helpful, especially for investors, as a trader you want to pay attention to the current day. Therefore, the historical patterns aren't as important to you as they will be to others.

2. Keep your education at the top of your list

This will be said again and again throughout this book because it is so important. You want to make sure that you do your research and are educated as a day trader before you take on your new career. Furthermore, you are going to continue to learn and grow once you start your job. When you create your watchlist, your education is just as important as it is for any other part of your day trading business. If you need to do more research to get a better handle on your watchlist, take the time to do this.

3. Remember your previous watchlist

You are going to create different watchlists throughout your trading career. It is important that you take note about each one of your watchlists in your trading journal.

You can always go back to a previous watchlist in order to help you develop a new watchlist.

Pay Strict Attention to Your Trading Plan

No matter how experienced or comfortable you become as a day trader, you always want to make sure you are paying attention to your trading plan. You will want to review your trading plan as often as you need to. In fact, some traders state that you should review it every day you sit down to make a trade. As I will discuss later, your trading plan will consist of three main parts: enter strategy, exit strategy, and stop-loss. Of course, you can make your trading plan as detailed as you feel the need to. You will want to create a plan that lays out your criteria for taking on a stock, your criteria for trading off or selling the stock, and then any plans on how you will limit loss if you find yourself in a bad trade.

Execute Your Plan of Action

Once you have developed your watchlist and reviewed your trading plan, you can then put your plans into action and begin your day. When you go in for a trade, you will want to make sure you follow your trading plan exactly as it states. If you find you need to make any changes to your plan, you can make this note for any future trades. It is important to stick to your plan because this will help you learn where your strengths and weaknesses are as a trader.

When is the Best Time to Make Your Decision?

One of the biggest questions you are probably asking yourself right now is when the best time to make the decision to take on a stock might be. While some of this will depend on what technique you are using and your own personal beliefs, the main reasons are probable movement and pricing. Like any trader, you want to receive the highest profit you can. Therefore, as you start to get into trading, you will find little tips and tricks within the patterns that will help you decide when to make your decision.

Your education will also help you when it comes to needing to make a decision. This is another reason why making sure you take trading classes, do your research, and get involved in online communities are so crucial. The knowledge you gain about day trading can come from all of these sources.

The key thing to remember is that you do *not* want to hold the stock overnight. You want to make sure that you close it out by the end of the day. However, once you take on a stock you never truly know if you are going to trade the stock within five minutes or at the end of the day because you have to. This is why taking the time to analyze the stocks before you decide to put them into your list will help decrease risks and give you a better chance of making a capital gain.

Chapter 3 - Building a Watchlist

Doing homework is important to a day trader. A wise trader once related learning how to trade to taking exams in school. He used to take a statistics class in school and it was a few days before the final paper. Everybody was allowed to bring in an A4 sized piece of paper where you can write all your formulae or comments on it and bring into the exam hall. It was like a cheat sheet of sorts. He didn't prepare for the exam but he managed to get hold of a photocopied version of the cheat sheet of the smartest student in class. Armed with that genius piece of work, he went in to take the exam. But during the exam, he could not do a single question. He didn't write the cheat sheet, and he didn't know how to use it at all. He didn't know how to apply any formulae and spent a long time just to find where a piece of information was written. He didn't go through the process of understanding why certain things were written down and certain things weren't. Only the person who personally wrote it will understand, and they are the type of people who do well in the exam. The same logic applies to trading. If you just blindly use somebody's strategies and watchlists and hope that you can replicate his success, you will be in for a rude shock during the actual trading. You have to understand the rationale behind each move and ultimately, you want to create your own plan which works for yourself. In this chapter, I will explain on how I form my watchlist and hopefully, you can understand some of the thought process that goes through my head as I find my stocks to trade.

Every morning, I want to enter the market with a clean slate and a well-formed plan. The best time to formulate this plan is doing research on the night before. The market closes in the afternoon and I always cultivate the habit of taking out an hour or two at night to review my trades for the day. This allows me to get better and better over time. A good portion of the time should also be spent to creating your watchlist. A watchlist contains a list of stock that you will probably want to play tomorrow based on your screening criteria. Usually, I create a list of not more than 10 stocks on my list the night before. In the next morning before the market opens, I will want to review this list and update it based on the pre-market action of the stocks. I can either take out those that are not trading according to my plan or add in more tickers who are setting up nicely during pre-market.

I like to trade NASDAQ listed stocks and selective NYSE stocks; I hardly ever touch OTCBB or pink sheet stocks due to the lack of volume and liquidity. I always trade using the one-minute candlestick chart and do not use any fancy indicators such as the MACD or the RSI. It is my philosophy to keep things clear and easy. NASDAQ provides the greatest liquidity and you can move in and out of the market relatively easy. To the surprise of many, I like to keep my stock screening process really, REALLY simple. I use 4 main indicators to determine if a stock can be traded.

1) Volume

2) Range

3) Support/Resistance

4) Chart Pattern

Volume

I look for charts that are in play with tons of volume. You want a *large audience* to be following the chart, because this way, support and resistance lines will become a self-fulfilling prophecy. Typically, a chart should have at least

1,000,000 daily shares traded for me to consider it. The volume should also have seen a spike in comparison with the past daily volume of the stock.

Range

The next criteria is range, I look for a stock that has at least 0.25 cents in range. Anything less than that is not worth the time because of how little the stock moves every day. Penny stocks are a different matter because of their low stock price. However, I usually don't trade these stocks unless they become really liquid and has seen a volume spike. A large range indicates to a trader that it is volatile and he can make a larger amount of money per share traded.

Support and Resistance

When it comes to using technical analysis, I do not over complicate matters. You might have learnt from other trading books about using fancy indicators like moving averages or Donchian channels. I don't use any of these. The only indicators I use for day trading are support and resistance lines. If you find that certain indicators seem to be working well for you already, then that is great. Stick with what you are familiar with and what seems to work for yourself.

Support and resistance lines are very important to determine if a stock can be traded. If a stock tries go higher and breaks past a point of resistance, there will be a surge in volume because everybody believes that the stock can surge and that is when the stock starts to trend upwards. However, it is not always the case. There can be cases of fake breakouts or breakdowns that trap people into thinking that the stock can trend in the anticipated direction. Eventually, if the stock chart refuses to move as expected, these people panic and the stock might spike in the opposite direction. It is important to have a plan in case they happen. Once a breakout on a long chart happened, I like to buy on the pull back or as the chart dips.

Entries are very important to a day trader when every tick counts. I don't like to chase a stock when it is at its highs because you never know when a chart may pull back and crash. Even though, eventually, it may rise back up and you may be correct, you save yourself the headache of watching the chart going against you.

Multiple Time Frame breakouts, Former Runners and Overextended Charts

When looking at the daily chart, I also look for multiple time frame breakout or breakdown. This means that the chart tests the line of resistance or support multiple times over a period of 3 to 6 months. When the chart finally cracks this line, the volume is typically much stronger than an intraday breakout. Of course, you can couple an intraday chart breakout together with a daily chart breakout, the chances of the chart trending strongly high much higher!

Another important thing to look for is if the stock is a former runner. Of course, just because a chart has spiked before doesn't mean that it should spike again, but more often than not, this is what people look for. If they see a chart breaking out and that it has spiked in the past before, they will be psychologically induced to believe that it can run again. This herd mentally can lead to these former runners spiking up again and this is what we want to take advantage of, whether on the long or the short side.

Overextended charts are daily charts that have been going up much at a much faster rate than previous days. This kind of chart gets on my watchlist because it is usually due for a quick pull back before deciding on the trend again. A lot of overextended charts ride on overly bullish emotions and therefore, we aim to anticipate a pull back for profit taking. It is NOT guaranteed to do what you hope it will, therefore, always make a plan for yourself.

How to Scan Stocks Using Finviz.com

Finviz.com is a great free tool you can make use of to do your daily scans and I use it every day. If you are thinking of using it often, it may be helpful to save your screen settings so you don't have to manually set them up every day. I do believe you have to create an account for this but the process is free and fairly straightforward.

I always sort my charts my volume in the descending order. This will show charts with big action and big volume in the first few pages. I will usually pass the stocks through 3 scans.

The first gives me stocks, which are very bullish. I want stocks that have big range and are moving up today. If the results are too many, you can narrow them down by adding more constraints. Similarly, if the results are too restrictive, I will take away the pattern and volatility option.

The second scan is the scan for bearish stocks. The settings are exactly the same as the bullish scan except that all indicators are showing down instead of up. In this kind of charts, we are looking for a continuation of downward trend or a temporary pull back.

The last type of scan is the breakout scan. I make use of the pattern scan and select horizontal resistance to find stocks that are testing horizontal resistance. This is a neat feature which I encourage people to use in case there are any potential multiple time frame breakout charts which may be of interest.

After I find the stock that I want, I will then copy their tickers out into a word document or notepad and that will be my watchlist!

Here are a couple of charts that interest me:

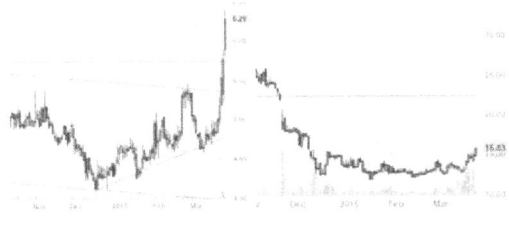

The first chart is a great example of an overextended chart where the price action speeds up as compared to previous days. Notice the obvious parabolic shape of the chart at the last 2 days. The second chart is also a nice example of a chart that has had a very bearish run and has put in a bottom. You can tell that because the chart has been testing support line at about $12.50 but did not crack below it. Instead, it picks up volume and starts to grind upwards.

How to Use the Watchlist

The watchlist is created so that you can have a better feel of the momentum of the stocks you want to trade on the next day. If you already have a watchlist written out, you save yourself the panic of looking through a whole list of stocks again. In the next morning after you have compiled your watchlist, you want to be looking at these stocks and look out for a confirmation of your trade idea. Is the stock moving in the direction as you anticipated it to be? Is a trend forming in your desired direction? If the stock is not moving how you think it should be, take it off your immediate watchlist at market open and allow the stock to set up throughout the trading day first. This way, you are actually narrowing down your watchlist to a few stocks that you are most confident about playing at the market open.

Chapter 4- Trading and Time

When one thinks of the different investment tools, if not the practice, of the investment in general, one cannot but considers the temporal factor. This is one of the factors that other miller discourages the trader. But why?

In these times, we are so used to the concept of *everything and immediately* we cannot wait any longer. We demand everything immediately, also losing track of time and the precious value of time.

Unfortunately, in online trading, you cannot expect to have everything and immediately, but above all, we cannot expect to become experienced traders and professionals in just under a month or worse than a week.

You cannot think of becoming an expert trader if you do not want to study and practice! In online trading, but also in investment, in general, it takes time to learn how to trade. Another advice that is not feasible at the moment is to think about spending some time to find a deserving, professional, and worthy investment and investment technique.

When trading, it must be done seriously and professionally. If, for example, we trade in a trading strategy based on currency trading, with a maximum payout of 65% for a positively closed trade, then we must enter the perspective that we must give money to work with a specific strategy.

If you are following the market trend, it will be counterproductive to exit the market because, in addition to losing its capital, you may not even get the desired return. That's why time is money, and it should not be wasted unnecessarily. Above all, hurry is a bad companion.

The time factor is also one of the main factors for which it is decided better to entrust its capital to a financial expert so that this is to make the choices for them. Very often, however, this trust is not always repaid by an increase in one's capital. Most often this capital is completely lost.

The Importance of the Right Time and Timing

Understanding when the right time to trade is very important. Giving money to mature is certainly one of the most determining factors for the success of your investment. The fundamental concept remains the same: within what you want to earn money and how to earn them.

To make sure that you know, in advance, how much you can earn and how to make money for us, you cannot rely on chance, and above all, we cannot expect to waste time but not even to demand everything immediately.

Everything has its time; also in investment, they have their right times and their importance. As you can see, even the right timing serves to give way to the investment, to make your own cycle, and to express that reasonable expectation. The right setup also serves your capital to survive in any situation, resist negative moments, and always have the strength to start again.

Avoiding Risks

To better understand the risks involved in trading in risky strategies, it seems right to remember those that are the right principles. Suppose you can trade $10,000 in a strategy that is 50% risk. This strategy was put in place to double the capital within a maximum of 3. Highly risky strategy from our point of view as it could result in the total loss of the entire capital. This operation is recommended only to experienced traders.

With this example, we have made you understand how these operations allow you to double or triple the capital within a few months but also how you can lose all your capital in a matter of months. In fact, by implementing these dangerous strategies, you will also see the account halved, or entirely burned, within a few weeks.

To understand everything better, let's take another example. According to your trading strategies, you have traded on a particular asset with a strategy and think that this can give you a return of 50% within a month.

To not fall into error, we advise you to set the opposite goal or try to ask the question: how would it be if in half a month you lost half of the bill? Here is therefore explained and understood in a simple and fast way on what is the right time, but especially those that are the wrong strategies not to be adopted.

Limiting Damages of Social Trading

Many wonder if social trading is the right strategy to avoid wasting time and earning, thanks to social trading. Before proceeding, we remind you that social trading is not a risk-free form of trading, even if the risk, in this case, is reduced. To trade in social trading, we believe it is essential to operate for a period of time between 9 and 12 months minimum. This is for one simple reason. Before choosing an investment system, you must see the performance for at least a year. In this sense, there is no need to follow a trader, 24 hours a day, 365 days a year, but only that you have to consult all the data of all the operations performed during the year, perhaps with the help with special tools that simplify reading.

Once you understand how to trade, but above all, you understand how much trading and who you want to trade in, you have to consider the risk that you are willing to run. Beyond this limit, it is advisable to leave it alone.

In most cases, the conditions that have led you to make a certain investment choice must have solid foundations so that the investment can yield. That's why a period of 12 months is a period enough to make you understand if your investment is right or wrong.

Chapter 5 - Finding the Top Day Trading Picks

Making a successful move in day trading is very easy when you know how to trade and what to trade in. Even with the best trading strategies at hand, you will still not make the best move if you have not been able to apply the right strategy to the right stock during a trade. That is why many day traders fail, because they are unable to locate the best trading opportunities in the financial markets even when they have the right tools at hand.

The good news is that there is more than one way through which one can find the best trading picks for the day, and this presents a good trading opportunity for every day trader out there. This is in fact what traders need to know, because with the right opportunity, you can be sure of a profit, however small it can be.

Ideas from news reports

If you want to benefit from this, you have to read financial news reports every day. These are an excellent source of information because they are easily available. Through such reports, you will get to learn about specific companies that you can target during your trading sessions. Some trading platforms provide news reports for their traders. If not, you can always find this information online. Some of the aspects of reporting you should pay more attention to are:

- The earnings reports of companies that you could be interested in. This is a great determinant of whether the stock price will change or not.

- The new developments.

- The insider selling and buying of stocks.

These are some of the things that will determine the price change of a certain stock.

Alternatively, you can watch financial news on TV. There are financial news channels that you can capitalize in to get information on a daily basis on what is happening in the financial markets. The advantage of this is that you get the latest news reports, therefore it is easy to know what is moving the markets every minute for a chance to make a quick decision. You can also benefit from tips on stocks from financial experts especially if there is an expected significant price change in a stock of your interest.

Learning from other people

There are so many day traders in the world today and these are the people that should come to your mind once you decide to start day trading. Learning from other people about the trade and how to spot a good trading opportunity is better than learning from financial reports and online tutorials.

You can for instance join a group of people like you who want to start day trading or a group of people who have been day trading for a while. Even if it will cost you some money, it will be of great benefit to you considering the kind of advice that you can get from people who have been day trading for a long time and some of the tricks and tips that you can learn from them in the end.

Alternatively, you can follow people who are day trading in social media to get to know what they are up to and also to benefit from some of the ideas and advice that they might have for new day traders. The best people to follow in this case are professional and successful day traders who have been day trading for a long time. There are so many day traders today and their presence in social media makes it even better. They can share their trades in real time in these social sites for free and this is the kind of information that can give you a good idea on what stocks you should be watching out for in the next trade. You can also talk to them if you want for advice and insights on the same.

Ideas from your trading platform

Trading platforms provide every kind of support and information that traders will need when trading and this can benefit you so much. You can set up alerts for instance in order to be notified in case one of the most important signals that is in line with your trading philosophy and strategy indicate a change in the stock price. Many trading platforms have these technical signals and you can choose that which you feel are the most important in order to set a signal in case it is time for you to make a move. Once you receive a signal, it will be easy to know if you will trade or not depending on the trading strategy that you are using.

You can also use your trading platform to screen stocks. Most of the new trading platforms these days have a stock screener as one of the tools that you can use in order to search for stocks whose prices are likely to change, then you can get ready for the chance to place a trade. This is an important tool to use for new traders who have no idea where to get started in trading.

Trading platforms also provide reports pertaining to the stocks that are trending at a particular time for your decision making. Traders receive notifications at all times to let them know the stocks that are hot and those whose prices are likely to change as per a certain criteria. With such information at hand, you can easily weigh your options bearing in mind the kind of trading strategy that you are using so as to know when to trade and the stocks that you can trade in.

Chapter 6- Trading Cryptocurrencies

Cryptocurrency is quickly growing in popularity. It is estimated that there are more than 1000 different versions out there, and they all work in different manners. For example, Bitcoin, one of the most popular cryptocurrencies and the very first one, is used just like the regular currencies you use on a day to day basis. Ethereum is more for startups who are trying to enhance the blockchain technology. And there are many other options that are out there, and they are used in different ways.

One neat thing that you can do with these cryptocurrencies though is to use them in day trading to help you to make some money in the process. Since there is a lot of volatility that comes with these markets, which means that once you learn how to work with the charts that each has, you will be able to benefit from the many highs and lows and ups and downs that come with these cryptocurrency markets out there.

In this chapter, we are going to take some time to look at a few of the day trading strategies that you can use for day trading to get the best results possible. Some of the different strategies that you can work with to use day trading on cryptocurrency includes:

Breakout

The breakout procedure is going to revolve around the idea that the cost is going to clear a predetermined dimension in your outline with some expanded volume. This strategy is going to have the trader go into a long position after the currency breaks above the opposition. Then you will again enter into a short position once you see that the currency breaks underneath it.

Scalping

You will find that scalping is going to work really well with this kind of security. There are a lot of trades that occur in this market on a regular basis. People all around the world are always looking to find ways to make more money from these markets, and there is a constant exchange between various other currencies and the cryptocurrency that you want to work with. Scalping will help you to make profits in the process.

For this, you will just watch for all the downturns that come with the market and then you will purchase the currency. Then you will move on to selling it as soon as the price or the value goes up. The most important thing to remember here is that there are going to be some fees for exchanging the currencies back and forth, so factor this in when you are looking to do this method to make sure that you will actually earn some profits in the process.

Steady incremental profit accumulation strategy or SIPAS

When you first get started with your day trading journey, it is always best to eliminate any of the wild swings or the unexpected fluctuations that will show up in the market. This is why it is often best to start with USDT and trading it to Bitcoin or one of the other altcoin pairs so that you won't end up with a lot of fluctuation concerns on both sides of your currencies. USDT is a good baseline that will not cause a lot of fluctuation either.

Assuming that the exchange you are using for cryptocurrency is going to work with USDT, and all of the major and reputable ones do, the goal for the day is for you to produce at least one to two percent from a few altcoins. You want to make sure that the altcoins have a history of stability over the past two or more days. This is going to help you to produce a profit that is at least 7 percent in a

12-hour period of time. If you do this over a week, you can earn more than 50 percent in profits.

In addition, if you are able to find an altcoin that has been doing some consolidation over the past few days, then this is a good option to go with as well. What we want to make sure we are avoiding here is big fluctuations to the price. Using this simple strategy can make sure that you stay on track and that you will profit from that initial investment in two weeks or less.

It is also possible for you to go for a higher profit than what we are talking about here. This isn't a problem and can be pretty easy but remember that the bigger the profit you want to earn, the more risk you add to it all. And greed is always going to result in a drain to your profits, regardless of how much knowledge you have about the market and everything else.

For the most part, the one to two percent increments is the best. If you are able to stick with these numbers, you will be able to avoid all of the big losses that can occur once the emotions, and a large amount of money, are on the line in that particular trade.

There is a lot of volatility that can show up in the market for cryptocurrencies, and it is important to really understand the market, to pick out one that has been relatively stable over the recent time, and then work with that one to do the right day trades that will bring in profit. If you can bring it all together, you will be able to make some good profits in the process.

Chapter 7 - Forex Trading

The foreign exchange currency market, more commonly written as the forex market, is the largest of all the investment markets, currently boasting more than $4 trillion dollars' worth of transactions per day, or roughly 10 times more than what the New York Stock Exchange can manage. Despite the lucrative potential available in this market, it was long outside the realm of the amateur trader as technological limitations made it difficult to amass the information required for such an undertaking. Luckily, the rise of the internet, along with countless online forex trading platforms, means that anyone who is interested can take advantage of the extreme leverage rates available in the market to turn a small initial investment into a serious payday.

Before jumping in with both feet, you are going to want to keep in mind the fact that the forex market is completely speculative which means that unlike in most markets when you buy and sell in the forex market you aren't actually gaining anything physical in the process. Unlike the stock market where you acquire shares in a specific company, for example, in the forex market, all you are doing is moving numbers around in various computer databases with relevant information relating to the countries in question causing them to either move in one direction or another. Your gains and losses are then expressed in the currency of your choosing.

If this seems like a bit of an odd system, that's because the forex market only exists because international organizations and countries needed an easy way to move currency around in massive quantities without going through the steps the average person would be required to do such a thing. These entities tend to trade in units of currency that are so extreme they can actually affect the overall value of the currencies being traded, which is where the speculative side of the market comes into play.

Generally speaking, only about 20 percent of the movement in the forex market is from these major entities, with the rest coming from investors that are trying to make a buck from the movement that spreads out through the market as a result. While a majority of these investors are professionals working for financial institutions or hedge funds, more and more private traders are jumping on the bandwagon each year, drawn to the promise of potentially huge wins thanks to the available leverage.

Forex facts

The most important thing to keep in mind when trading in the forex market is that each forex trade is actually a pair of disparate trades because you are always selling one currency in order to pay for another. Forex trades are made in three separate sizes, known as lots. A micro lot is 1,000 units of a given currency while a mini lot is 10,000 units of a currency and a standard lot is 100,000 units of a specific currency.

When the market moves, the smallest amount that is tracked is known as a pip which is one percent of the total price of the currency in question. When you are first starting out in the forex market you are going to want to avoid taking on trades that are larger than a micro lot as in this case the pip is worth 10 cents of the currency you are working with. This means you won't quickly lose your shirt when a trade turns against you in the last moment. If you stray to mini lots or standard lots you run the risk of losing $1 or $10 respectively, per pip. For reference, you can expect a trending currency to move around 100 pips per trading session.

While the forex market differs from other markets in key ways, it is important to always keep in mind that it is the same in the ways that matter the most as it is driven by supply and demand as much as any other market. This means that when a certain currency is in high demand then the value of that currency will naturally continue to increase until the point where the market has more sellers than it does buyers, at which point the price will start to drop until the buyers start to bite once more.

When trading in the forex market it is extremely important to be aware of instances where a specific currency is about to increase in demand so that you can jump on it as quickly as possible. This means you will want to keep abreast of things like economic predictions related to world powers, current geopolitical strife and key interest rate movements. It is important to keep in mind there is no such thing as insider trading when it comes to the forex market, as such anything you learn about is fair game.

Another important fact to keep in mind is that the forex market never closes from Monday to Friday, it just shifts its focus. While closed on the weekends, during the week the market naturally shifts its focus between various currency pairs based on the portion of the world that is currently the most active. For example, the currency pair USD/JPY would be active during the portion of the day when the US is active and again when Japan is active. The forex market is divided into three segments based on the time of day in the US, Asia and Europe. This isn't anything that is strictly regulated, as the forex market isn't regulated in any traditional sense, rather it is simply more profitable to trade a specific currency when it is the most active.

While you can likely find someone willing to buy or sell into any currency pair imaginable, there are 18 primary currency pairs that are traded most of the time. These pairs are made up of only eight different currencies which means you should aim to be familiar with each of them if you want to find any success in the market in the long-term. These are AUD the Australian dollar, CAD the Canadian dollar, CHF the Swiss franc, EUR the euro, GBP the British pound, JPY the Japanese yen, NZD the New Zealand dollar and USD the US dollar. Knowing the currencies you can safely ignore early on is crucial to making your early forays into the market as successful as possible. There will always be time to mix things up at a later date after you have mastered the basics.

Lack of traditional regulation

As already noted, the forex market is not regulated in nearly the same way as other markets and is, in fact, considered an unregulated exchange. This essentially means that when someone chooses to make a trade dishonestly they are not going to be at the mercy of any regulatory body which means it is up to the community to dish out justice. As such, every trade in the forex market is based on what is known as a credit agreement which essentially means everyone operates in good faith. As anyone who breaks the agreement will never be able to trade in the forex market again, it tends to work fairly well in most instances.

In addition to this system, the US also has what's known as the National Futures Association which is a voluntary organization that forex dealers can join which holds its members to a higher standard than the market as a whole. It also offers arbitration options if a disagreement does occur. This means that when you are dealing with a Forex broker or dealer in the US then you are certainly going to want to ensure they are an NFA member.

As there is no one to enforce such things, the rules are more relaxed in the forex market as well. This means you are free to short sell as much currency as you have access to as long as you think you can make a profit off of it. On the other hand, there is also no limit to how many lots you can buy in a single trade which means you could make a billion dollar trade if you had the cash.

Finally, the number of traditional forex brokers are few and far between which means that a majority of forex transactions don't require a commission fee. Rather, forex dealers make their money off of the spread which means it is likely going to be a bit larger than what you may be used to. This means the forex market is principal only which means the dealers are taking on just as much risk as the traders. As such, it is impossible to buy on the bid or sell at the offer when trading in forex; however, this limitation is mitigated thanks to the fact that it can be much easier to make a profit when trading in the forex market as commission and fees don't come into account.

Currency trading facts

When trading in the currency market, the currency you are selling is a short position and the currency you are buying is a long position. As an example, if you make a trade of EUR/USD then you are going long on dollars while going short on euros which means you are selling euros and buying dollars.

As noted above, you really only need to focus on a handful of currencies in order to get a full understanding of the basics of forex trading. As such, when you are taking your very first steps into the market then you will want to focus on USD/CHF, GDP/USD, USD/JPY and EUR/USD. In addition to these pair, you will want to keep an eye out for the commodity pairs, so named because the related countries tend to move commodities around in large amounts. These include NZD/USD, USD/CAD and AUD/USD. Finally, with the addition of EUR/GBP, GBP/JPY, and EUR/JPY, you have more than 90 percent of the trades made on the average day covered.

Reading a currency quote

Regardless of the currencies, you are working with, they will all be quoted in a specific way. The first half of the currency pair is referred to as the base currency while the second is referred to as either the counter currency or the base currency. As a general rule USD is the default base currency and gains tend to be written in dollars per the other currency and when they are quoted will include both an ask price and a bid price.

The bid price is the amount the forex dealer will ultimately be willing to purchase the base currency for, and it will be written in an amount of the secondary currency. Alternately, the ask price is the amount that a dealer can expect to sell any base currency for and is typically written in the counter currency. The difference between the bid price and the ask price is where the spread comes from and is typically written out to the fourth decimal place.

Don't forget margin and rollover

In order to trade in the forex market successfully in the long-term, you will need to take margin into account in a different way than you would with other markets.

Specifically, in the forex market, your margin ceases to be a down payment on potential future equity and is instead best thought of as an account deposit that can be accurately used to help mitigate losses related to forex trades that may go south down the line. Generally speaking, the greater the leverage a dealer allows, the greater the margin on the trade is likely to be.

When it comes to completing a required forex trade, the general rule is you must complete your side of the trade within 48 hours. This period of time can be extended, however, through the use of a rollover which pushes the due date back a full 48 hours in addition for a percentage of interest paid on the transaction. A rollover can be used multiple times, though the fees are cumulative so it is important to track them closely for the best results. Rollovers are also trade in the forex market just like currencies.

When taking advantage of a rollover transaction, it is important to keep in mind that the difference between the interest rate of the base currency and the counter currency can be properly visualized via an overnight loan. When utilizing this type of loan, a trader will hold onto the long position of a currency based on the assumption that it has a greater interest rate to gain an advantage from. The amount gained from the rollover will then vary day to day depending on the interest rate's variance. If this all sounds too complicated, avoiding a rollover is easy, all you have to do is avoid holding any positions overnight.

Leverage

When trading in the forex market you can think of leverage as money that is being borrowed expressly for the purpose of potential increasing returns should a given trade go according to plan. While not advisable for those who are first getting into the forex market, you can easily find rates of greater than 100 to 1 which means it is possible to gain the benefits of trading a lot while only having the cash on hand to pay for a micro lot. It is important to remember, however, that if things don't go according to plan then you are going to be on the hook for a lot's worth of loss so trade carefully.

As such, it can be effective to think of leverage as magnifying the movement of the market as a whole. Some of the losses that you could potentially experience when using leverage can be mitigated through a fastidious use of stop losses or through the use of a margin watcher. A margin watcher is a type of software program that comes with a variety of online trading platforms and allows users to set parameters to ensure that their losses are never going to be any greater than they absolutely have to be.

Chapter 8 - How to pick stocks like Warren Buffett

To recap, growth stocks are stocks that may not necessarily have strong fundamentals. Regardless, the stock market, for better or worse, somehow fell in love with these stocks. If you need a great example of a growth stock, take a look at Facebook or Tesla. Compared to other companies with stronger fundamentals, it's usually a no-brainer comparing the stocks of these high flying and heavily hyped companies with more solid companies.

In normal times, people would pick stocks that have zero to no debt, solid sales growth, industry domination and solid management as well as tremendous cash flow. Unfortunately, or fortunately, depending on your perspective, the stock market values stock primarily in terms of perceived growth potential. This is how stocks like Twitter were able to achieve some traction early on before gravity pulled them back down to earth.

One big danger with growth stocks is that, eventually, the stock market may fall out of love with you. That's the bottom line. When that happens, reality hits. It's as if scales fall out of people's eyes and they notice the huge amount of debt the company has. They start noticing that the company only has two or three major customers. They realize the company's cash flow over a four-quarter period actually goes through some tremendous turbulence.

Unfortunately, if you're one of those investors who realize this later on after the stock has tanked, you're pretty much a day late and a buck short. Keep this in mind when it comes to growth stocks.

I don't mean to discourage you but we need to be clear as to what exactly we're looking at. These are not, generally speaking, fundamentally strong stocks.

With that said, one of the techniques that I will teach in this chapter involves using fundamental analysis to pretty much separate growth stocks in terms of likely winners and probable losers. Before we begin, let's do a quick recap.

What are Growth Stocks?

Growth stocks are shares of companies that appreciate faster and higher than general market indices like the Dow Jones Industrial Average index.

For example, the Dow Jones Industrial Average appreciates 20% year after year, you can bet that growth stocks leave that in the dust. We're talking maybe doubling in a year or possibly doing much better. Whatever the case may be, there is a big black and white difference between general index performance and growth stock performance.

Also, when you pay attention to the other stocks in these growth companies' industries, they leave everybody behind. It's as if they are the Cinderella story of their particular industry.

Again, Tesla Motors is a good example of this. Usually, when people think of the automotive industry in the United States, they think of companies like Ford, General Motors, and others. But Tesla shines in this industry. It's as if gravity doesn't work on that stock. It seems that the normal rules that hold back and drag down automotive stocks don't apply to Tesla. It's as if investors hold it to a different standard.

It's easy to see why, because the resume of its CEO, Elon Musk, is more reminiscent of Silicon Valley and its high-flying tech stocks than Detroit and the old industrial

America that pretty much characterizes the US automotive industry.

Also, when you look at the specific underlying technology of Tesla, you really can't say that it is purely an automotive company. If anything, it's an electric motor vehicle organization.

With that said, Tesla is a growth stock because its rate of appreciation sets it apart and puts it head and shoulders above its competitors, both in its industry as well as in terms of the general industrial average. Keep this in mind when determining which stock, on its face, is a growth stock and which stock isn't.

Invest in Growth Stocks to Grow Your Wealth

What good are growth stocks for? If you are faced with two opportunities: investing in a solid company that dominates in its industry, has solid cash flow and is never in the red, or a company that just got started and admittedly gets a lot of media hype and love, which should you choose?

Well, it really boils down to what your objectives are. If you are looking for long term growth because you are investing your retirement money, chances are, you should go with solid companies with solid fundamentals. These are companies that are not going anywhere any time soon.

On the other hand, if you're younger or you just graduated from college and got your first corporate job, your objectives and mindset might be different. You might be in a hurry to grow whatever you managed to save in your 401K or IRA plan. If so, you might want to take a long, hard look at growth stocks because they are great for quick portfolio growth.

How much growth? We're talking about out-pacing the general market indices. Whether you're comparing your stock's growth to the S&P 500, the Nasdaq or the Dow Jones Industrial Average, you can bet that if you pick the right companies, you can get solid returns.

Before you get too excited...

It's easy to understand the concept of growth stocks but picking out the right stocks is another matter entirely. So how exactly do you tell which growth stock is worth investing your hard-earned dollars on?

What makes this complicated is that it's often hard to spot brand new growth stocks. These are stocks that, for the longest time, were just plodding along. They're basically just another company in the crowd. Not that many people are paying attention to them. Maybe only a handful of analysts would track their stock. All of a sudden, they start getting a lot of love and attention from the rest of the stock market.

It's hard to get in on growth stocks right at the point of ignition. It's easy to get in when they've already appreciated quite a bit. For example, Apple Computers was pretty much on its deathbed at certain levels during the period when Gil Amelio was the CEO of that Cupertino, California-based computer giant. The interesting thing about the Amelio period was that only a few people remember it. It was a time where Apple stocks were basically on life support.

And one of the best things that Apple did at that time was to buy out Steve Jobs' company, Next. Apple wanted Next not because of its computers, which was sold through a very narrow education-based marketing channel, but because of its operating system.

It turned out to be the defining point in Apple Computer's corporate history because the second act of the Steve Jobs era brought the iPod, the iPhone, the iPad and key innovations that blew up Apple stock to the stratosphere. But you would not have seen that coming when you saw how Apple's stock performance was plodding along at the end of John Sculley and Gil Amelio's leadership periods.

This is a classic example of a growth stock. If you owned Apple stocks at its lowest point at that period, you'd be a very, very wealthy person today. Apple has just basically blown up ever since that point, thanks to the amazing growth made possible by the iPhone.

I tell the story of Apple because it's easy to relate with that story. We're talking about a real company with real products producing real changes. Make no mistake about it, for better or worse, the iPhone and the age of consistent Internet connection changed the world.

Indeed, it was a fulfillment of CEO Steve Jobs' challenge to John Sculley when he hired Sculley from Pepsi. He said, to paraphrase, "You can spend the rest of your life selling sugared water, or you can change the world." And sure enough, Apple Computers changed the world.

Now, it's easy to see how Apple would be a growth stock, but I've got some sobering news. The vast majority of growth stocks out there are not of the same caliber as Apple. A lot of them are simply creatures of hype or market reputation. Whatever the case may be, the dollars that you make when you buy these stocks low and you unload them for a high price is all too real. In other words, you make the same real dollars trading these stocks as if you had traded Apple stocks.

The key here is to buy the right stocks before the rest of the market recognizes that the stock that you're buying is actually a growth stock. This is how you position yourself to become wealthy. As the old saying goes, you make your money when you buy.

Usually, when people think about earning a profit, they think about making the money when they unload. That's wrong. You make your money when you buy. In other words, you recognize value that is unnaturally low or isn't being fully recognized by the rest of the market. This is the same philosophy that animates Warren Buffet's investment strategy. It's all about looking at unrecognized or unappreciated value.

How do you go about picking the right growth stocks?

Step #1: Compare stock growth over the same time frame with a broad index

For example, you're trying to determine out of a basket of 100 stocks which of these would make for a growth stock. You look at their individual performance over a fixed period of time and find the broad index growth rate. Whether we're talking about the S&P 500 or the Nasdaq or Dow Jones Industrial Average, it doesn't really matter. You would see which of these in a basket of 100 stocks grow at a very decent rate compared to the index.

Step #2: Compare stock growth over the same time frame to their industry's average

Now that you have filtered your initial basket of stocks, the next step is to look for their industry's indexes and compare their stock's growth over the same time frame. Again, after this step, you should be able to filter out some stocks from your list.

Step #3: Consistent stock growth over a significant time frame

What constitutes a significant time frame? Usually, 3-5 years is a good comparative time frame. Don't get too crazy with extending this too far back because the company, 5 years ago, might be a fundamentally different company and it would not make much sense to compare the company now to what it was before.

Maybe it was in a different industry, maybe it was run by a different CEO, maybe it had a different philosophy. Whatever the case may be, 5 years is a good enough time frame. Extending it way past that period might be counterproductive.

The key here is just to find some sort of consistency. We're talking about quarter over quarter growth, both in sales, earnings and stock price.

Step #4: Filter by P/E

Now that you have a fairly short list, the next step is to filter your list based on price per earnings ratio. A price per earnings ratio, as I explained earlier chapter, divides a company's current stock price by the amount of earnings per share the company has.

For example, if a stock is making $10 per share of profit and its current stock price is $200, its P/E is 20. Now, what is the upward limit of your P/E filter? 40 is a good cap. If you find a stock that is beyond 40, you might want to skip it.

Usually, the lower the P/E, the more attractive the stock. Anything under 40 means that there is still a way to go for the stock to appreciate. If you are looking at a stock that is already at 40 or close to 40, it's pretty much maxed out. Unless, of course, its earnings continue to grow at a healthy clip. This earnings growth could justify a higher stock price.

Step#5: Compare growth stock candidates among the percentage of institutional owners

This filter requires you to get to the nitty gritty of the company's SEC filings. The US Securities and Exchange Commission requires public companies to make a public filing of their percentage of institutional owners. In other words, how much of all their stock holders are pension funds, mutual funds, investment banks and other professional institutional shareholders. At this point, you're going to try to filter based on percentage of ownership. The higher the percentage, the better.

The reason for this is actually quite simple. When an institution buys millions of stocks in a company, it usually locks in a fairly long period of time-especially if they get a decent return. In other words, they don't freak out like an individual investor and liquidate their positions just because the stock experiences hiccups

Usually, they would stay for quite some time due to bureaucratic and institutional reasons. This provides quite a bit of stability. At the same time, this also makes the stock more attractive to other institutional owners because, usually, institutions tend to behave with a herd mentality. If they see that a lot of "smart money" is investing in one particular company, a lot of them would also want invest. But since they hold billions of dollars in assets, you can see that they can move quite a bit of stock and this can lead to some serious appreciation due to the volume involved.

Step #6: Consistent sales growth

Pay attention to a potential growth stock's financial filings. Look at whether its underlying sales are actually growing year over year. Usually, 10% appreciation is a nice benchmark. The more the better. What's important is its consistency.

In other words, it's okay if a company isn't appreciating 10% or more year after year in sales growth, as long as it is marching forward. In other words, in one year, it's 10%, and then it's 11% and 12% and so on and so forth. There can be dips, but as long as it's over a 10% threshold, this is a good sign.

Steer clear of companies that have flat sales or sinking sales. This can indicate a lot of things. Either they only have a small number yet high-volume customers, or their industry is changing. It may well turn out that it's only hype or reputation keeping the company's stock up.

Don't be the investor who is left holding the bag when you bought in on hype and it turns out that the company's sales have been haemorrhaging for the past few years. Again, when doing sales growth analysis, keep it within a time frame that's manageable like 3-5 years.

Step #7: Track earnings growth

Look at the sales growth at Step #6 and pay attention to the total earnings of the company. Does it keep up with sales growth? Does it have a decent tracking with sales growth or does the company's earnings and sales go on opposite directions?

Step #8: Decreasing or low debt

Pay attention to how much debt a company has. Again, by law, American public companies release this information, so you should look into the financial statements of the company and look for its debt load. In particular, pay attention to its year over year debt level. Is it decreasing or does it maintain a fairly low amount of debt? On the other hand, is its debt load swelling?

Extra Research

Just in case you haven't tired of the 8 Steps listed above and you still have a lot of spare time, here is some extra research that you should do in determining whether your initial basket of potential growth stocks yields some gems.

Is the company a market leader? Pay attention to its market and see whether it's in the top 3. Analyze its industry and try to figure out if the industry is growing or undergoing a massive sea change.

Keep in mind that, thanks to technology, a lot of industries have been disrupted. For example, the compact disc industry is fairly small compared to its former self. The same applies to all sorts of optical media like DVD discs. Pay attention to the state of the industry. Is it undergoing disruption or is it growing?

Also, pay attention to the branding of the stock. As I've mentioned earlier, oftentimes, what separates a high-flying stock from what would otherwise be a solid company that doesn't trade all that well is the amount of media mentions it has and how much the rest of the market has fallen in love with that stock. Pay attention to its brand. Does it have a solid brand? Is there massive market buzz?

Usually, when you detect this, this is reflected in the stock's price already. However, if you notice that there's not much market buzz around the company's products or it has few media mentions, you might have a gem in your hands if it has solid brands and a low stock price. You might be looking at an undiscovered or fairly obscure growth stock that may have a breakout point in the future.

Next, pay attention to its product line. Does the company have new products in the pipeline? How important are patents in the company's industry? Are we talking about a company that basically has mature product lines that may even go off patent? Pharmaceutical giants are the first ones that come to mind when it comes to this type of analysis.

Finally, does the company look like it's poised for market domination? Does it have a certain sub-niche that we can reasonably say it's either poised to take over or it has already taken over but the market hasn't caught on yet?

Again, with all these filters that I've given you, you should have more than enough to go with in terms of figuring out which company it might be on the brink of a nice stock breakout. Breakouts happen when the rest of the stock market starts paying attention to a company because the market finally wakes up to the tremendous amount of value the company brings to the table.

The next step, of course, is to buy in and hold growth stocks for short term to mid-term gain. The key to growth stocks is you should not hold them forever unless they have become blue chip stocks or they have really solidified their position that they make for great fundamental long-term plays.

Remember to Switch From Growth Stock to Growth Stock

Keep in mind that what makes a growth stock a growth stock is the fact that there's a tremendous amount of market buzz around it. Please understand that the party is not going to last forever. The love affair is probably going to be short lived. Do yourself a big favor and be ready to switch from growth stock to growth stock.

You're chasing after return on investment. You're chasing after appreciation. You're not necessarily falling in love and getting married to the stock. It's not a long-term commitment. Be ready to hit the exit button.

The bottom line with growth stock is actually quite simple. You're just trying to hitch a ride on different stock's growth rate. If done right, don't be surprised if your portfolio appreciates by double digits or even triple digits year after year.

Chapter 9 - Developing Your Target Price

One of the most important factors that you need to be considering does not only pertain to understanding how day trading works as a whole. In addition to developing a concrete strategy for yourself, you also need to be considering how you should be entering and leaving the market. How are you supposed to know when's a good time to enter and when's a good time to exit? This chapter will focus on three key beginner entry strategies that you can use at your disposal. These include learning how to interpret what's known as candlestick charts, understanding level II quotes, and understanding what to take as important from the stock market news. Once you understand what's going on, this type of information will be able to help you know when the market is prime for entry.

Additionally, some of the terms that are presented in this chapter are thrown around in the stock market on a daily basis, and if you're behind on the lingo then you're going to have less of an idea of what's going on. There are far too many days trading terms to be able to condense them all into one chapter. For this reason, be sure to be on the lookout for my advanced guide to day trading that follows this book in sequence.

How to Find a Target Price

Before we take a look at specific strategies that you can be implementing for your day trades, we're going to examine the different types of target prices that you can set for yourself. A target price is the price at which you would ideally want to both sell and purchase a share of a particular stock. There are various ways that you can go about identifying your target price, and deciding on one ultimately is a decision that's made based on your overall trading strategy and style. Of course, you are going to want to have a firm process in which you purchase your stocks, and the different ways to find your target price can help to accomplish exactly that.

Target Price Technique 1: Momentum

The first price targeting technique at which we'll look involves finding "momentum" from news stories and other types of press releases. A common technique that is often used by traders who are implementing momentum involves picking up a stock when a news story about the company is hot, and then trading it when the story takes the company into what is known as "reversal". Reversal just means that the stock is now moving in the opposite direction from what it previously was. Another type of momentum-focused strategy that some traders use involves the price of a particular item. If you remember the example that we used to discuss supply and demand in a market, this type of momentum works similarly to that. As the volume of a product begins to decrease (or rather when the supply is disappearing), the investor knows that it's time to move on to the next trade.

Target Price Technique 2: Daily Pivots

For this technique, the investor will be looking for a sign of reversal in the stock's price throughout the day. The goal of the investor when he or she is using the technique of a daily pivot is to purchase the stock when it's at a low-price point and sell it when it's at a high price point. Seems simple enough, right? In this way, the investor is preying upon the volatility of the market, or rather how much the price of a stock will vary throughout the day. Volatility is typically defined as the measure of the range of the stock's price within a given period of time. The greater the volatility, meaning the greater the difference between the lowest price and the highest price, the more profit (or loss) potential there is.

Target Price Technique 3: Fading

Fading is when the target price is determined based on when investors who were not previously purchasing the stock begin to buy it again. Fading as a concept is closely related to the concept of shorting stocks. Shorting a stock involves purchasing a stock at a high price and then selling it at a lower price than which you originally bought it. After you've sold it at the lower price, you then purchase it again when it's priced higher and make a profit from this difference. Short selling is involved in the technique of fading because as an investor who is using fading, you are basically targeting people who are eager to be in a particular market once more. The types of investors who you are going to attract when you fade include those who were once scared out of the market for a particular share or stock for some reason and those who are early buyers looking to get to a particular market before others see the trend. The types of stocks that people who are using the technique of fading purchase are usually those that are overbought, because people are eager to pick up these stocks due to a saturated market.

The notion and implementation of fading can be risky because if you miscalculate the market, the idea of the short stock can potentially backfire on you. You'll have sold your shares at a low price with no hope of seeing a profit in the future. On the other hand, fading can also be pretty rewarding. You're essentially preying on people who feel as if they're missing out on a hot market, but the advantages to this method certainly outweigh the potential ethical discrepancies. Remember, the stock market is a cut-throat kind of place. Any way that you can get ahead, without cheating, is fair game.

Target Price Technique 4: Scalping

If you've ever been to a baseball game and have seen people standing on the street selling after-market tickets, then you have already been acquainted with the notion of scalping. Scalpers at sporting events are trying to make a profit any way that they can, and their ultimate goal is to walk away with any type of profit that they can. Moving back towards the stock market, when a day trader uses the strategy of scalping, he or she is looking for any profit that exists. The strategy here is pretty simple. As soon as the investor sees even the smallest profit emerge on the market, he or she sells the stock immediately. This particular strategy is especially popular amongst day traders because of the fact that it's pretty easy to implement. As a day trader, you're going to have a bunch of stocks that you are going to be watching all the time. Instead of looking at complicated charts and trying to figure out if you're making the right decision, the technique of scalping can help you to eliminate any of that. Additionally, scalping is great because it can disassociate the investor from becoming too emotionally invested in any one stock. Instead of purchasing a stock and desperately hoping that it will grow astronomically, taking any gain from a stock even when it's small will help you to stay emotionally unattached.

Chapter 10 - The AutoTrading Function Explained

One of the most important functions of the MT4 platform is AutoTrading. Nowadays, almost eighty percent of trades during a day are automated.

That means that robots, not humans, are executing a trade. Now, before saying that you don't use automated trading, think of any stop-loss or take profit orders you set. Or pending orders that are considered mandatory in disciplined trading.

The MT4 executes them automatically, without human intervention, when the market reaches certain levels.

But the MT4 AutoTrading function really refers to something else.

The rise of trading robots or algorithms is best seen in the currency market.

Ever noticed how the market suddenly spikes or dips on releases of important economic news? That happens because robots are instructed to buy or sell based on the outcome. And they initiate those trades all at the very same instant.

Most robots belong to so-called quant firms. An essential part of high-frequency trading (HFT), such algorithms use sophisticated formulas to trade thousands of times per second. Sometimes even more.

The race is on, therefore, for the best execution, because the one that is first to the market will get a competitive advantage.

Retail traders can't build algorithms to fully compete with the HFT industry. However, they can build programs to buy or sell automatically based on instructions.

Such programs, called Expert Advisors, run smoothly on the MT4 platform. They are easy to use and monitor, provided you can get access to one.

This part of the book assumes there's already an Expert Advisor or robot available. If the trader has some programming experience, you can open the MetaQuotes Language Editor simply by pushing the F4 button with the MT4 platform launched. There, you can program your own robot and save it on your PC.

If you don't have the programming skills yourself, outsource the job and find someone to program it.

The AutoTrading function is accessed from the main MT4 window.

See that black rectangle? The little red dot shows that currently no Expert Advisor is running.

Even if there is an Expert Advisor or robot attached to a chart it won't trade until the AutoTrading function is ON. So, make sure you double- and triple- check that the indicator shows green.

The Expert Advisor must be imported into the trading platform. Under the MQL4 folder, look for the "Experts" folder and paste in the robot file.

Remember to close and re-start the trading platform for the changes to take place. Next, look for the Navigator window. You can find it by clicking the toolbar icon shown in the black square below (a file folder with a star on it).

A long list of the available indicators appears, and you could select one of those this way. But for now, we want the Expert Advisors. The one you just installed should already be there.

So go to the Expert Advisors folder at the bottom of the list and click the + to expand the folder.

Two Expert Advisors are already included with the default installation. We'll use one of them only for the purpose of illustrating how to apply and run a robot on the MT4 platform.

Expand the Expert Advisors folder that appears on the left side of this page and you'll see one of the robots has the name Moving Average.

To apply it to a chart, simply click and drag it on the currency pair and timeframe. In this example, it's the EURUSD daily chart.

A dialog box will open. The "About" tab is always there to describe the robot, the copyrights, and so on. The really important tab is "Common".

Here, you have the option to tell the robot to trade either in both directions (long and short) or in one direction only.

This can be a useful feature when trades remain open overnight.

Some currency pairs pay a negative swap, meaning there's a cost for keeping positions open for a day or more. This option tells the robot to buy or sell only, or do them both.

The "Allow live trading" must be checked. If it's not, the robot will not run, even if the AutoTrading button on the main MT4 window is pushed on.

Clicking OK and the popup window disappears, but the robot is up and running. How do we know that?

Check the top right on the chart above. See where it says Moving Average? That's the Expert Advisor's name, and the MT4 tells us it is applied on the chart.

The smiley emoticon confirms it is running smoothly on the background. Basically, it monitors incoming data to decide if a desired trade appears or not, according to the programming.

When the emoticon doesn't smile anymore, something is wrong with the robot. It stops trading. For instance, if the

AutoTrading tab isn't ON, or selected, the emoticon won't "smile." Hence, the robot isn't trading.

To remove an Expert Advisor, just click anywhere on the chart where the robot is running. From the Expert Advisors menu item, select Remove, and the MT4 will remove it from the chart.

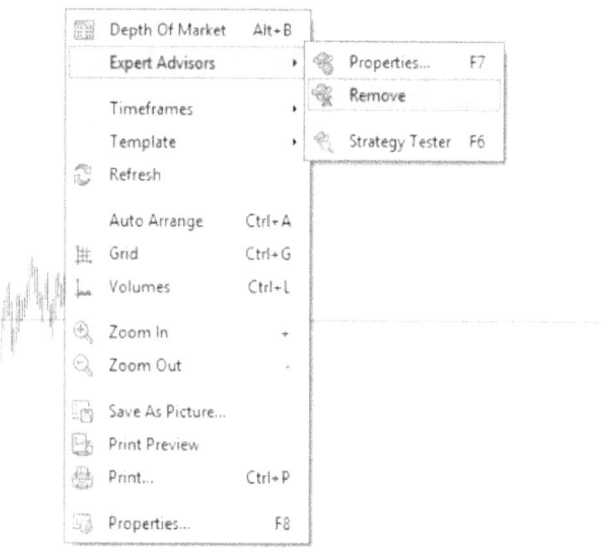

Advantages and Disadvantages of Using an Expert Advisor

Despite many traders believing there are only advantages of using a trading robot, reality begs to differ. As a matter of fact, the pros and cons list is quite balanced.

On the pro side, the obvious advantage is availability. A robot trades 24/5, without getting tired.

As long as the market is open, it scrutinizes the timeframes in search of the conditions that trigger a trade. People can't do that, as we need sleep.

One important detail here: Not everyone lives in a time zone where the market is active during waking hours. For instance, we know by now that the London session and the start of the North American session are more active than the Asian one.

What do you do if you're living in Asia and the market just doesn't move while you're awake? One answer is to put a robot to work while you're sleeping.

Running a robot means not missing any possible trade. That's the main advantage of it.

Also on the pro-side: the emotional roller coaster doesn't exist. Traders have an easy-to-go mindset about a trade, knowing the risk and the reward, and what it means for the trading account.

That's a key reason why many traders prefer to use a robot rather than trade on their own. They just can't face the pressure of deciding on their own when to get in and out of the market.

On the con side, running a robot comes with some costs. First, there's the cost of building and setting it up. If the trader doesn't have programming skills (and 99% of traders don't), building it costs money. Plus, the strategy is shared with a third party, which, in many cases, is a big issue.

Second, the trading platform runs the Expert Advisor only as long as it remains open. The moment that it closes, the robot stops trading. Think of a power failure, for instance.

Using a VPS (Virtual Private Server) solves this issue, but costs a monthly subscription.

Using a VPS is essentially renting a computer on a computer farm and accessing it via a remote protocol. After accessing it, traders can use it like the computer is in front of them.

After opening and setting up the MT4 on the remote computer, traders just leave the trading platform open.

The VPS provider makes sure the computer will never turn off, so that the robot trades 24/5, no matter what.

But another disadvantage comes from the difference between back-testing and live trading. Many times, traders are puzzled when a trading robot is profitable under testing conditions, but not when it runs on a live account.

The main explanation is that market conditions differ. But it also can be the result of different conditions in different trading accounts. There is no guarantee that an Expert Advisor will have the same results on two different accounts or on two different brokers.

Let me give you an example. If the trading robot is active on the four-hour timeframe, the closing value of the candlesticks can easily differ from broker to broker.

This is because depending on where the broker's server is located, the candlesticks can have a different closing price for the "end" of that day's trading. Hence, everything can differ, from the closing price to everything that indicators might calculate. Therefore, your robot's trading results will vary too.

Execution slippage affects results as well. Most of the trading accounts today, via STP (Straight-Through-Processing) and/or ECN (Electronic Communication Network), promise to execute the trade when there is a market.

But the broker can only execute the robot's orders to buy or sell according to the actual market, and when the market moves too fast the trade may be opened but not necessarily at the desired entry or exit price. In many cases, there's a difference between the entry calculated when back-testing and the actual live environment.

Another difference can result from variable spreads. If the trading account uses variable spreads (which most do), the spreads widen considerably during certain moments in the trading day.

This is evident especially on pairs with low liquidity such as the Canadian pairs, for instance. And spreads can get particularly wild at roll-over time.

But the robot won't know what to do if it isn't instructed to stop looking for a trade unless the spread meets specific conditions.

Sometimes there are specific market conditions that are too risky to trade with a robot. For instance, the SNB (Swiss National Bank) decision to drop the EURCHF peg from the 1.20 level.

As it turned out, many retail traders had their stop-loss orders just below the 1.20 level and many of those positions were being handled by Expert Advisors.

The market reaction was unprecedented under the relatively new ECN (Electronic Communication Network) and STP (Straight Through Processing) technologies. Prices effectively disappeared, and for a few minutes there was simply no market.

A robot or Expert Advisor doesn't know what to do in these kinds of situations. It will continue to trade, ignoring potentially catastrophic events as though nothing happened.

Another example is the Brexit vote. The United Kingdom decided to hold a referendum regarding its European Union membership.

Because the polls indicated deep uncertainty and a close tie among voters, Forex brokers began sending emails warning traders that the market conditions could change. In the aftermath of the SNB mayhem, brokerage houses began to warn investors ahead of potentially volatile events.

Now, the trader has the option to stop the Expert Advisor and pause auto-trading until the event goes away. In other words, trading with a robot in extreme market conditions isn't recommended. For this reason, most retail traders use a robot only to scalp for tiny moves on the lower timeframes, instead of for longer-term investing or swing trading.

Nevertheless, even with all the cons, many traders find it more rewarding to use a robot. Everything can be set up in such a way to overcome and protect against most of the negative aspects.

However, traders need to know ahead of time what to look for. And that's why we wrote this book.

Chapter 11 - Intraday Candlestick Pattern

One method day traders use to analyze stock movements is called a "Candlestick." This tool helps you visualize a stock's movement and try to interpret the meaning of that movement. A candlestick is made up of the share's opening price, closing price, high, and low for a stock over a single day. By following the relationship between candlesticks over a period of time, an investor can get a sense of how other investors are feeling about that stock. Remember, day traders make up a modest number of investors and shares traded in a stock. There are plenty of others investing in a particular stock who have different objectives than you do. A mutual fund may hold a large position in a particular stock as part of its portfolio for a year or longer (funds that are set up to mimic a particular stock index such as the S&P 500, may hold a particular stock for as long as it's followed by that index). The point is movement in a stock's price fluctuates because of the actions of stockholders in general and not because day traders effect price swings.

When using this method, the trader draws one candlestick for each day's trading, and then compares the candlesticks to draw an understanding of the market's views of that stock. Keep in mind, this approach does not give you any indication of why the market views a stock a particular way. In drawing a candlestick, use green for growth and red for decline. Your drawing should look like a candle with a wick at each end. The height of the candle is determined by the amount of distance between the stock's high and low for the day. A tall green candlestick would indicate a strong upward movement; a short one would indicate a much smaller change. The opposite would be true for a red candlestick. The longer the candlestick, the greater the decline that stock has experienced. The "wicks" show the relationship between opening and closing values compared to lows and highs. The bottom wick records the share's opening price (which is why it begins at the bottom of the candle), and extends downward from there. The top wick begins at the closing price (or top of the candle) and extends upward to the stock's high for the day. Learning to read the wicks (sometimes called "shadows") can help you understand more about the stock's movements over time.

Candlestick Pattern -- Bearish

Let's say you've decided on a particular stock. You look at it for the past few days and notice it's followed a rising pattern for three days in a row and then things changed. Suddenly, it's gone from a long green candlestick, to a short green one, followed by a long red one that rises above and below the previous day's candlestick. This "engulfed" look, indicates that investors are becoming more interested in selling the stock than buying it. (A decline in stock price means investors are "bearish" on a stock, while a rise indicates they are "bullish." The terms are used to convey stocks that are sluggish [like a hibernating bear] versus charging [like an angry bull].) The pattern created by this trend is sometimes called "A bearish engulfing pattern."

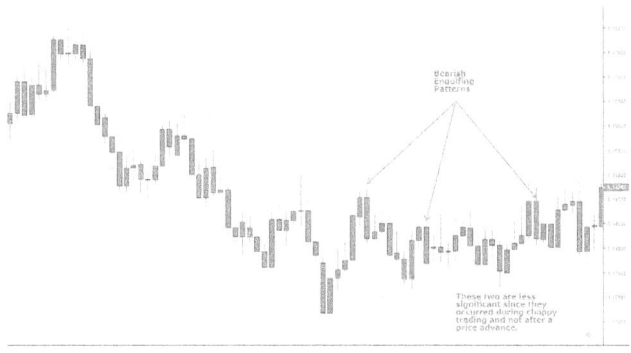

Candlestick Pattern -- Bullish

Of course stocks can also have a "bullish" pattern. In this case we have a downward trend in our candlesticks. They're red in color, and each day's beginning is lower than the previous day's. If you see a short red candle after several days of downward movements, followed by a longer green candlestick that engulfs the short red candle; you've found a "Bullish engulfing pattern.

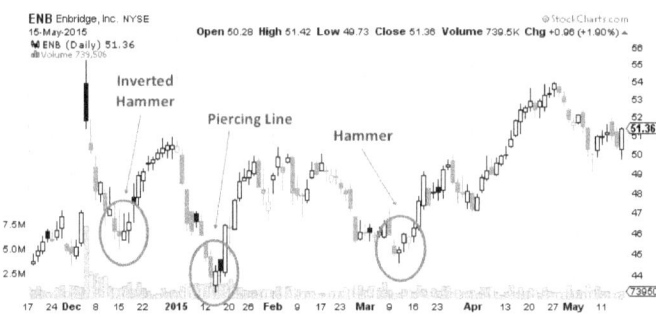

Candlestick Pattern – Evening Star Bearish

Sometimes in the candlestick pattern a small red candle will mark the peak of a stock's upward growth. When this happens, the small candle is called a "star". If a long red candle that opens lower than the star's bottom follows the star, the pattern is known as a Bullish Evening Star. The start indicates that stock buyers haven't purchased enough shares to move the stock price past the previous day's high.

The long red candlestick that follows can indicate that sellers are replacing buyers.

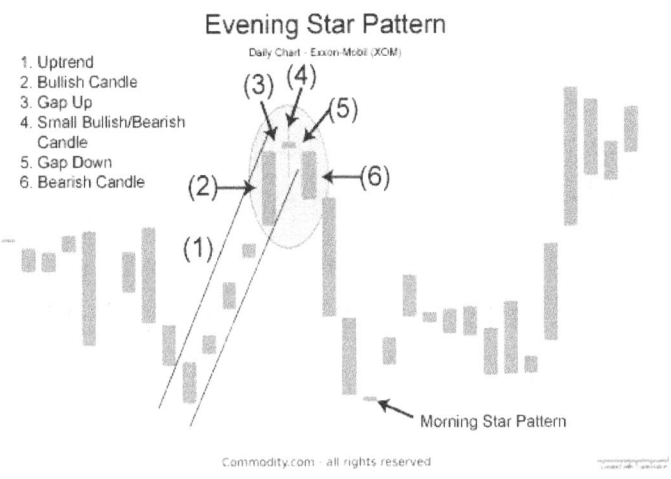

Candlestick Pattern – Morning Star Bullish

The reverse of the Bearish Evening Star occurs during a downward trend. In this case, a short red candlestick (the "star") is preceded by a long red candlestick. If the star begins lower than the previous candlestick's open, it becomes a stronger indicator. To complete the Bullish Morning Star trend, the start must be followed by a long green candlestick whose open begins higher than the star's open the previous day. If the green candlestick has a short lower wick, you have a stronger indication of the Morning

Star. This pattern is interpreted to mean an upward trend in the stock's pricing.

Keep in mind, these are patterns and not cause and effect. In the stock market it's very possible to have candlesticks indicate one thing, and then have something unexpected (bad news for instance) completely change the stock's direction even though the candlestick pattern contradicts that direction. This is why relying on a pattern system alone without paying attention to other stock indicators can be risky.

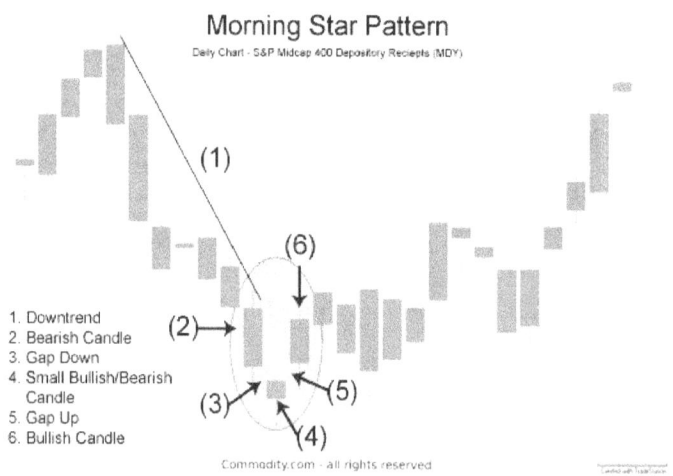

Chapter 12 - Bollinger Band Bounce Trading Strategy

Generally speaking, it is always going to be easier to trade based on an existing trend than it is to trade when one or both of your currencies in a pair is either rangebound or moving horizontally. This can be so difficult for many traders that they simply refuse to trade when the market is in this state and simply sit out the market until they can track down a stronger trend to follow. This only causes them to lose out on potential profits in the long-term, however, as there are still plenty of ways to make money without a strong trend to follow.

The Bollinger Band Bounce strategy is one such option, as it was created based on the way the price typically behaves when the Bollinger bands detect a limit when it comes to the range of movement the price can see in the short-term. Essentially, what this means is that the Bollinger bands have more elasticity than they normally do. In this type of scenario, the price frequently approaches the outer band before meeting with resistance and snapping back towards the opposite band.

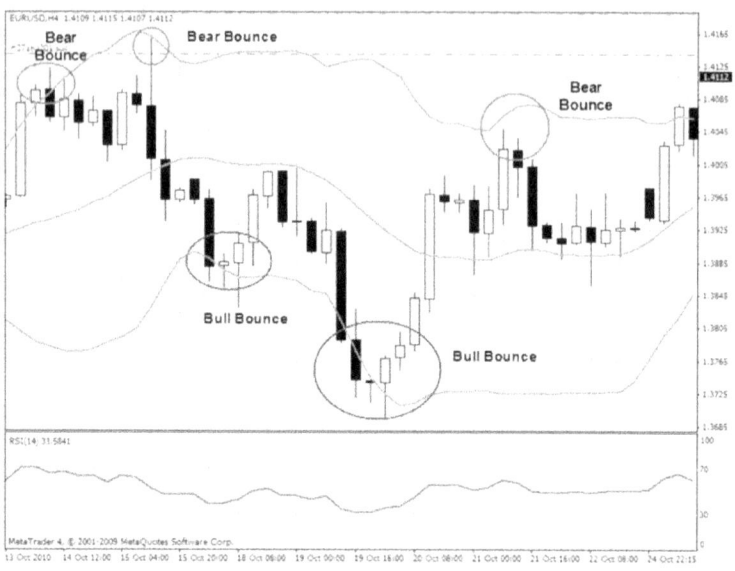

After you have noticed this type of behavior taking place, you can then make excellent use of it by simply trading based on the action of the price as it moves back and forth between the outer bands. While this is not an especially useful strategy if the market is moving vigorously in one directly or another, it is a great way to scalp in a market that really isn't doing much of anything.

Start off right: In order to make the most out of this strategy, you will want to start by determining that the price is actually range bound. To do so, all you need to do is to use Bollinger bands to ensure the price is staying put, specifically on the same side of the middle Bollinger band each time it returns to that point. Assuming the price continues to rebound in the same way, then you can expect the existing trend to continue until this is no longer the case.

Tweezer bottom candlestick

One of the strongest indicators that the market is ranging is when a tweezer bottom candlestick pattern emerges. If this happens at the same time as a Fibonacci retracement, resistance and support level or relevant pivot level, then you will know the signal is almost too strong to contain. If this is the case, then you will be able to make a profit from trading at this level rather than waiting for the confirmation of a ranging price based on the way it reacts to the opposite band as you normally would.

This pattern is also easy to spot as it is actually made up of two different, separate, forex candle patterns. The first candle, known as the setup candle, is either going to be notably bullish or bearish and will ideally occur at the tail end of a substantial price push down. This candle represents the last vestiges of the downwards price surge and also a failure back from the low price.

The second candle is known as the confirmation candle and is always going to be bullish. The confirmation candle will have a peak price or lower wick that will match quite closely, or even exactly, with that of the setup candle. The stronger the signal, the greater the length of the confirmation candle wick. This represents the amount of low point rejection that is taking place.

Fundamentals to keep in mind: The tweezer bottom candlestick pattern is going to most commonly occur at the end of a trend towards decreasing prices, regardless if this is part of a larger trend or simply a short overall retracement. If this takes place at the end of a long-running price decrease, then it likely indicates that the supply of sellers is just about to run dry.

This then naturally means that the market of buyers who are eager for opportunities is going to be primed for action and more likely to jump into the market as the levels of the currency pair in question appear quite cheap. If there is a bear and bull struggle taking place as well, keep in mind that it is likely the bulls will come out on top. After this happens, the price will often settle near the higher point on the confirmation candle as well as at a point that is above where it started.

The tweezer bottom is also more likely to occur during a positive trend that causes the price to retrace to that of a previous support level. This will also cause some downward movement in part due to buyers striving to make a profit while at the same time sellers who are slow to move into the market in part thanks to inflated prices and in part simply because it is easy to see the overall number of buyers drying up. This, in turn, often causes the price to decrease to a level when buyers will once again be interested. This, eventually, will cause the price to be pushed up once again.

Generally speaking, in order to maximize the value potential from this situation, you are going to want to purchase a buy stop at a point between two and five pips above the highest price the confirmation candle has reached so far. If you are extremely confident about the state of the market, you could also choose to place an order that is at market. Regardless of your choice, you are still going to want to place a stop that is anywhere between two and five pips below the bottom most point of the tweezer bottom candlestick.

As always, this advice is simply a general guide as the current level of market volatility is going to play a huge part in where you place your stops. If you are working with a longer timeframe then setting a stop that is up to 20 pips below or above the current price is a perfectly viable strategy. The greater the size of the bullish confirmation candle, the greater the likelihood that the price is going to increase. This is only true up to a point, however, as if it is too long then you might have a difficult time finding an adequate risk and reward ratio.

As an example, if you set a stop loss that is 50 pips below the tweezer bottom just to manage the trade correctly and you know that there is resistance at 20 pips above the current price action then you can consider the trade to have a low possibility of success and pass on it.

Engulfing candlestick

In order to confirm the signals that you find in the bouncing Bollinger band strategy, you will want to be on the lookout for either bearish or bullish engulfing candlestick patterns. You can also look for an evening star. This type of candlestick pattern is made up of a pair of forex candles, both the confirmation and the signal are going to be contained within the second candle which is known as the confirmation candle. You will be able to recognize it due to its large body that completely consumes the setup candle. At close, the confirmation candle will have a lower overall price than the setup candle.

This type of pattern often starts near the top before continuing upward regardless of whether that move is connected to a retracement or a longer trend. If it appears at the end of the protracted price increase, then this is a signal that the supply of buyers is filling out the seller's market. Assuming this occurs, more sellers than ever are likely to jump on the bandwagon thanks to the high price of the currency pair. With one focused move, they then defeat the buyers by exceeding the bullish effort found in previous candles and reversing the price in the process.

You can also find a similar pattern in a downward trend assuming the price temporarily retraces to a predetermined resistance level. This typically occurs when a variety of different sellers all take their profits at once and buyers move in to rapidly take advantage of the deflating pricing. This can also occur as part of a normal period of market exhaustion. This, in turn, causes the price to move upward to a level where sellers can once again be reasonably interested in the currency and start pushing the price in a downward direction once more.

Bullish engulfing pattern: The bullish engulfing pattern is also made up of two separate candles, with both the confirmation and signal found within the second candle. In this pattern, the setup candle is bearish and typically occurs after a hard-downward price push. The second candle is also going to be bullish and contains a body that essentially engulfs the setup candle. The closing price of this candle is also greater than the setup candle.

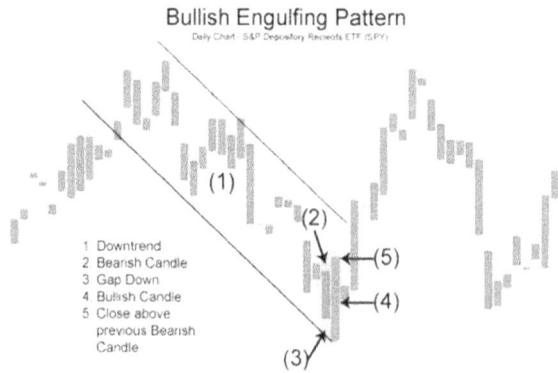

Bullish Engulfing Pattern
Daily Chart : S&P Depository Receipts ETF (SPY)

1 Downtrend
2 Bearish Candle
3 Gap Down
4 Bullish Candle
5 Close above
  previous Bearish
  Candle

The bullish engulfing pattern tends to set itself up at the bottom point of a downward price trend and typically signals that sellers are in low supply and the market is starting to favor buyers. This will attract new buyers who like the cheap price. In a concentrated push, they then overpower the sellers and exceed the bearish leaning, reversing the direction of the price.

Assuming this scenario forms during an uptrend, the price will naturally retrace itself to a support point and the downward move will cause additional sellers to take advantage of the high prices. This, in turn, will also cause the price to gently move in that same downward direction until the buyers are once again willing to bite. When this occurs, the price will move upward once more.

Limits and the bouncing Bollinger strategy

Once you have a clear idea of the type of indicators you are going to be on the lookout for, the next thing you are going to want to do is to take into account the mechanics surrounding this strategy's stop loss, entry, and take profit limits. When considering these limits, it is important to remember that this is a scalping strategy which means that your goal should be to enter immediately once the signal can be positively confirmed. Additionally, you will want to use a tight, aggressive stop loss and also a take profit limit that is set to the opposite of the mid-Bollinger band.

Once the move has been confirmed successfully, the next step is to move the stop loss to the breakeven point immediately to prevent an additional loss. If you miss this part of the process then you can find yourself losing out on profit if the price bounces off the middle band and then retraces before you can clear a profit, taking out your stop as it goes. This can happen in the first part of the trade as well, assuming you don't immediately move the breakeven point as soon as it is safe to do so.

There is no ideal time limit when it comes to moving the breakeven point and learning when to do so in order to maximize your profits will only come with practice. If you move to quickly then you will likely find that you are stopped via the expected retracement, even if the price is still actively moving in your direction when you initially move it. You will need to remain vigilant so that you don't miss your chance, without making the mistake of rushing either.

Generally speaking, this strategy is best used when the market is experiencing a lull which means no news announcement or the like are expected anytime soon. Furthermore, you are going to want to avoid using it on pairs that are prone to spiky price action. Finally, you are going to want to ensure that you aren't committing to this strategy just because the price reaches the outer band, additional verification is going to be required to ensure that this is the right move.

Chapter 13- First Hour Trading

The truth of the matter is that, while the market is open all day long, the majority of the trading that occurs will do so either during the first hour of the day or the last. As such, new day traders can make things a lot easier on themselves by starting off exclusively focusing on the first hour of trading. When done correctly, sticking to first hour trading will allow to generate enough liquidity to get in and get out as soon as the market solidifies for the day. Studies show that the market only continues to trend roughly 20 percent of the time which means that most of the time the market won't be doing much of anything. This type of strategy does require a good deal of volume in order to be successful, which means that it is best undertaken by those who have at least $100,000 worth of investment capital available to start with.

First hour breakdown

Opening 5 minutes: The 5-minute chart is by far the most common chart that day traders refer to and this starts from the first 5 minutes. This is enough time to start seeing volume and price of various stocks start to spike as gaps start to form based on the differences between yesterday's close and today's open. You will often be able to get a general idea of what is going on in this arena from news or announcements that break or are rumored to break in the early morning hours.

The rules and parameters for the day have not yet codified, however, so this period of time is also one of the most volatile of the entire day. The gap from the previous day makes establishing a range impossible which, in turn, makes trading during this period akin to little more than gambling and there are certainly easier ways to gamble than via day trading. All told, you will want to be aware of what the market is doing in this time frame but avoid interacting with it yourself if you don't like the idea of gambling with your money.

Between 9:30 and 9:50: While this segment might seem a little non-traditional, the fact of the matter is that there are numerous reasons to jump in prior to the 10 am segment and the first of which is the relative lack of competition. By making a move at before the hour you will get the jump on those who are waiting for the full 30-minute chart as well as the latest 15-minute chart, while at the same time only increasing your risk a modest amount as things have typically started to settle down at this point.

This is the time you will then want to determine what the low and high values for the morning actually are as this will help you determine the types of clearly defined price points that indicate boundaries on the stock you are considering. If the stock in question then moves past the points you have established then you can safely assume that they are showing the beginnings of a trend. Once these trends have been established you will then be able to determine if it is going to be more profitable for you to trade with the trend or against it.

Between 9:50 and 10:10: This is the time period where you are going to want to make a bigger move based on the results from the first 20-minute period. This is the period of time when you are going to want to enter all of your trades for the day if you are trading the first hour as if you wait until 10:15 am, or later, then you will be severely hampering your ability to make a profit even if you make all the right decisions up until this point.

Between 10:10 and 10:30: During the final 20 minutes of the cycle, you are going to want to let the stock smoothly follow the trends that you noticed early on. While this might not seem like much, the reality is that if you got in at 9:50 am, then 10:30 am is 40 minutes which can make for a lot of time for movement during the early part of the day. You will be able to realistically wait until as late as 11:00 am if things are really moving well, though at the first sign of slowdown you are typically better off getting out. It is important to never just let your morning trades run on cruise control as you never know when things might switch directions, destroying your profits in the process. Remember, the odds that things will continue moving in your favor enough to make a real difference once things have slowed for the day are much lower than the state of the market changing and costing you money instead.

During the last 20 minutes you are going to want to be paying close attention to the signs that it is time to get while the getting is good. It is important to know what you exit goal is before you get started to ensure that you aren't too busy worrying about working out the details that you actually miss the signals you were looking for.

Instead of being worried about missing out on every single dollar that you could possibly earn on a trade, it is much more productive to worry about losing out on existing profits instead. Make a point of setting profit targets for all of your trades and then once you hit them, get out when the getting is good. Over time, you will find that if you guard your existing profits, rather than pinning over the profits that might have been, your results will be much more reliable. If you hit your target, but the movement on the underlying stock is still so prominent that you hate to miss out on what could be a significant additional windfall, the right choice may instead be to split the difference.

Specifically, you would then want to sell off half of your shares before setting a new stop loss at the current price so that you will be able to cash out the other half for a profit no matter what. You will then want to set a new price target for the remaining shares and repeat the process as needed. While you may not make as much as you ultimately would have if you had kept all of your shares, at the same time you prevent yourself from losing out on all the profit you have already made which is more important in the long run.

Chapter 14 - Momentum

In stock indicators, momentum measures the rate of the fall or rise in stock prices. From this perception of trending, momentum is a necessary indicator of weakness or strength in the price of the stock. Based on historical data, momentum is proven more useful during the upward trend in the market compared to a downward market.

The main reason for this is that the markets follow an upward trend than they follow a downward trend. To put this simply, bull markets have the tendency to last longer in comparison with bearish markets.

Technical analysts utilize a ten-day time period to measure momentum. You will often see the zero line in most charts. When the most recent closing price of the stock is more than the closing price for the previous 10 days, the positive number from the formula is plotted on top of the zero line. Meanwhile, if the latest closing rate is lower compared to the closing rate 10 days ago, the negative measurement will be placed under the zero line.

In taking the measurement of the price differences over a certain period of time, you can begin to take note of the prices at which the stock is falling or rising. Momentum can help you identify the trend lines.

Specific trend lines can develop as the price of stock increases, while an upward momentum plot line on top of the zero signifies that a rising trend is strongly developing. If the plot line is beginning to level off, this signifies to technical analysts that the latest stock price is about the same as it was 10 days ago. Hence, the trend's velocity is slacking. The reverse situation can also be true.

As a beginner in day trading, you should understand that if the momentum indicator slides downwards under the zero line and then will reverse in a rising direction. This doesn't mean that the falling trend will be completed. This can only mean that the falling trend is also slacking down. It is also true if the plotted momentum is on top of the zero line.

Below are several techniques, which you can use to become more successful in momentum trading:

Entry Techniques

To determine the inertia in the market, day traders can use EMA or Exponential Moving Average to find the downtrends and uptrends. If EMA rises, the inertia will favor the bullish market, and if the EMA falls, the inertia will favor a bearish market.

In measuring market momentum, the trader can use the MACD (moving-average-convergence-divergence) histogram. MACD is an oscillator that displays a slope showing the changes of power between the bears and bulls.

If the slope of the MACD shows uptrend, the bulls are becoming more dominant. If the slope of the MACD shows downtrend, the bears are becoming more dominant.

The impulse system will issue an entry indicator if both the momentum and inertia signals are moving in the same direction, and the exit signal is issued if these two signals become divergent.

If the indicators from both the MACD and EMA are pointing in one direction, the momentum and inertia are working together towards the obvious downtrends and uptrends. If both the MACD and EMA, the market is bearish and so a downtrend is imminent.

Below is a sample chart showing an MACD with 9-period EMA.

Exit Techniques

The primary reason why momentum trading is effective in both strong and sloppy markets is that you are searching a short-term momentum and not a longer one. Financial markets usually trend within any week, and the ideal stocks to trade are those that are regularly showing strong intra-day trends. In this case, you should take note to step off the momentum before it peaks.

The MACD for the day is often the first to turn, as the rising momentum starts to weaken. However, this may not be a genuine selling indicator of the removal of the buying indicator. In using the impulse system, this indicator is not enough for selling.

Take note that if the weekly trend is falling, and the daily MACD and EMA are falling while you are in short position, you must cover the shorts as soon as possible for the indicators to stop a selling indicator, if the downtrend momentum has stopped the fasted part of the descent. The best time to sell is before the trend reaches the absolute bottom. In contrast with a selected entry point, the exit points will require fast actions at the particular moment that your determined trend will appear the nearing end.

Conclusion

Mental strength and concentration are crucial if you want to use momentum in day trading. This will allow you to stay steadfast if things are moving as expected and wait once the targets are ready to be achieved. Day trading using momentum also requires strong discipline, a unique trait that makes short-term momentum among the most difficult strategies of making profit.

Chapter 15 - More Trading Strategies

In this chapter, we will continue our look at commonly used day trading strategies. We will begin by looking at what is known as ABCD patterns, bull flags, reversals, moving averages, support, and resistance, and then finally Bollinger bands.

ABCD

The ABCD strategy is a basic strategy that looks for a certain pattern in stock to get an idea of what the trend is in the market. What you are looking for is a stock that starts low and rises to a high point A, and then drops back down to a low point B. Point A represents the breakout level, that is if the stock passes point A, a second time during the trading day you're expecting it to rise significantly, representing an opportunity where you can sell for profit. So why would point A drop down? This is a point when many investors have decided to sell because they are happy with their profits and they are leery of the stock continues to increase.

As the stock begins to be sold off, at some point it will reach a low point, which will be point B in the chart. The low point occurs when new buyers overtake sellers that began selling as a result of the stock reaching the high point A. Then, when more buyers come in the stock will settle on a new low point, C, which will be higher than point B. If this pattern is established, you take your risk level as point B. After it hits point C, it may begin moving upward again. This is a signal of a good buying opportunity so we may jump in at this point. If the ABCD pattern is realized, it will move up to a new high point D, where we can sell and take our profits.

In the chart below, if the stock goes above point A, this is considered breakout. Time to consider selling. This is a bearish ABCD, which means you see a time to sell and take profits before the stock drops again. Point B could you're your stop-loss point. This is a bearish ABCD, meaning we expect it to drop.

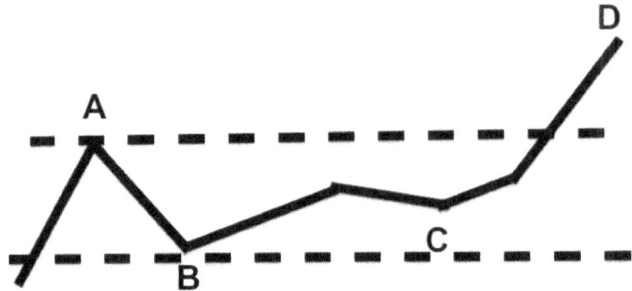

Example- suppose that XYZ Stock opens strongly, going from $50 a share up to $60 a share. Then over the next hour, it drops to $40 a share. It then rises up to $55 a share and drops a little bit to $53 a share. At this point, we will consider buying. Our risk level is the lowest point which was $40 a share. If the stock starts turning upward, we buy. So, we can take any point between that and our purchase point as a stop-loss, so, for example, we could set a stop loss at $45. It then continues upward to point D, say in this case it rises to $63 a share, where we sell to take our profits before the stock drops again.

We can also have a bullish ABCD pattern. This is where the stock looks to rise.

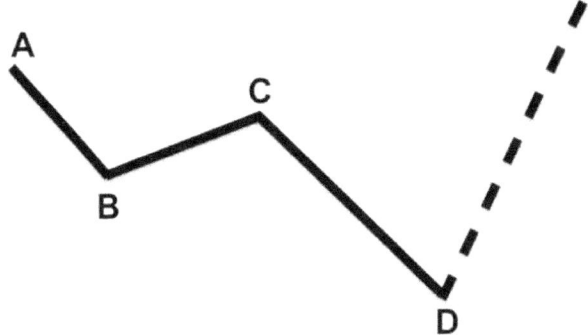

In this case, we buy at point D. This can be done buying calls or actually going long on the stock.

When we see ABCD patterns, the lines AB and CD are known as the legs. The line BC is either called the correction or the retracement. A retracement is a temporary reversal of the stock price. In that case, the stock has an overall upward trend for the day. So, the retracement is seen as a temporary downturn that is going to reverse. A correction is a downturn of 10% or more in the price of the stock. A correction is an ideal time to buy a stock because odds are it's going to go back up and possibly strongly so. In the second chart, at point D there has been a correction. In the first ABCD graph, we see a retracement, on the way to an overall upward trend.

Ideally, the lines AB and CD should be of equal length.

The Bull Flag

A bull flag is a strong upward trend in the stock. However, after shooting upward, the stock enters a phase of consolidation, when people slow down or stop buying, but before a new rise may begin. The "flag pole" is a steep rise in the price of the stock over a very short time period. The "flag" is a time period when the price is high but stays about the same. A bull flag is a symbol of a buying opportunity for a stock that has already shown a significant increase. You should set your desired profit, buy and then sell when it begins increasing again up to the point where you have set to take your profit. You should always include a stop-loss, a bull flag is no guarantee and the price might actually start dropping.

When there is a bull flag, it is bordered along the bottom by a level below which the stock is not dropping, known as the support. On the top, there is a level above which the stock is not rising. This is called resistance. Eventually, the stock is going to break out of the resistance so you want to buy before this happens, as the stock may see a rapid rise again. A bull flag may occur multiple times during the day as the stock trends upward.

The Bear Flag

A bear flag is equivalent to a bull flag but when a stock is tanking, so it represents opportunities to short the stock or buy puts. In this case, the stock will drop by a large amount over a short time period. It's going to have an upside down flag pole, and then a flag at the bottom where the stock stays within a narrow range for a while, bounded by resistance and support. This is a buying opportunity if you are looking to short the stock so you can buy a put with an appropriate strike price. The hope here is that the stock will continue it's a downward trend when it breaks out of the flag. It may do so rapidly and then hit another flag later in the trading day.

Reversals

A reversal is a major change in the direction of the price of the stock. So, the trend completely shifts and moves in the opposite direction. In order to look for reversals, look at the candlesticks on a stock market chart. The body of the candlesticks and its size relative to the previous (to the left) candlesticks is what is important. First, let's consider a signal for a reversal where a declining stock price is going to be going up in the future. If the candlestick of the most recent time is larger and fully engulfs or covers the candlestick to the left, and it's the opposite color, i.e. a green candlestick following red candlesticks, this indicates a reversal of a downtrend into an increasing stock price. This is a good time to go long or buy calls.

On the other hand, let's now consider the case where the stock price is going up, with multiple green candlesticks in a row. Then it is followed by an engulfing red candlestick. This indicates a reversal so we will expect the stock price to begin going down. That is, this is a point where we should short the stock, or if trading options invest in puts.

The larger the engulfing candlestick, the stronger the reversal signal is. That indicates that the change in direction has a significant conviction behind the reversal, which is the confidence of investors, larger volume and the price will change in larger amounts over short time periods. If the wicks engulf the wicks of the previous period, that is an even stronger signal that a reversal is underway.

When using reversals as a trading strategy, you need a minimum of five candlesticks in a five-minute chart. Then look at the relative strength index, which helps you evaluate overbought or oversold stocks. The RSI ranges from 0-100. At the top of an uptrend, if the RSI is above 90 that indicates that the stock is overbought and is probably going to be heading into a downturn. On the other hand, if you are looking at the bottom of a downturn, if the RSI is 10 or below, this indicates that the stock is oversold. That could be a signal that is about to see a price increase.

When looking for reversals, indecision candlesticks can be important in combination with the other variables discussed here. An indecision candlestick indicates neither an upturn or a downturn. That is if you see a downturn followed by several indecision candlesticks, that could mean that the stock is about to turn upward again. Or vice versa – if an upturn is followed by several indecision candlesticks, that can indicate a reversal resulting in a downward trending stock price.

Looking at the wicks can be important as well. When the lower wick of the candlestick is longer, that may indicate that the price dropped over the period of the candlestick, but the stock turned and was bought up. On the other hand, if the candlestick has a long wick at the top, that may indicate that the stock was bid up too much over the period. Traders lost interest and began selling off the stock.

At any time there appears to be a reversal, a trend of indecision candles or stagnation represents a buying opportunity no matter which direction the stock may be trending. That is if you are in the midst of a downturn and the stock is moving sideways, then it may be a good time to go long on it or buy calls. The opposite is true if the stock is at the top of a potential reversal. If it's moving sideways, it may be a good time to invest in puts. Keep in mind that this does not always work. The best indicator is whether or not a green (red) candlestick following a red (green) candlestick which engulfs the candlestick to the left is the best indicator of a coming reversal.

Moving Average

Another trading strategy that can be exploited is the moving average. This may help when a trader is looking for entry and exit points while trading. First, we will look at the simple moving average crossover strategy. Look at candlestick charts when considering moving averages with a two-minute interval.

You can include multiple moving averages in a chart with different periods. A faster-moving average on a chart is colored red and a slower moving average is colored green. A buy signal is a red line moving above the green line. That is, it breaks above the green line. A sell signal is when the green line is above the red line. If the lines are overlapping, then that means to wait. So, to profit, when the faster moving average tops the slower moving average, you go long, which means buy the stock or buy a call option. Then when the red line (or faster-moving average) goes below the slower moving average that is a sell signal. If you went long you sell your stock. It could also be an indication to buy puts.

A stop loss should be five or ten percent below the moving average line.

Solid profits can be realized when the stock breaks out high above the moving average. You can choose to take a half-position at this point, in order to lower your risk.

Following the moving average leaves your investments exposed to the markets for a longer period of time. If you are a beginner to day trading, this can increase your risk. For that reason, many beginners avoid following the moving average. It will be necessary if looking at moving averages to stay exposed to the market for several hours. On the other hand, some beginners will prefer this method, because you have more time to make decisions regarding your trades. One of the things that you will need to learn when day trading is that you have to think fast on your feet. If that is something that causes you an issue, using moving averages can help you get more attuned to the markets while utilizing a slower method. Large gaps in entry and exit points can also be an advantage, helping you get a nice profit on your trades that helps wipe out the commission fees.

Bollinger Bands

Bollinger bands are a very popular indicator for day traders, looking for price actions and indicators for strengthening or weakening. These were developed by none other than John Bollinger. Bollinger bands are adaptive trading bands. A trading band is simply a range of prices for security (aka stock). In particolar, Bollinger bands represent:

- Volatility

- The extent of price movement

- They indicate trend lines defining support and resistance

Bollinger bands are calculated using standard deviation. However, you don't need to be an expert in statistics to understand how Bollinger bands are calculated or what they represent. In short, a Bollinger band is calculated relative to some average of prices, for example, the moving average over a given number of periods. What the Bollinger band represents then, is the spread of prices about that average.

Bollinger bands only measure closing prices and how to spread out they are. Typically, they measure the 20 periods moving average, but they can be used for 50 or 100 periods.

Bollinger bands are dynamic. You will see them around the candlesticks in a stock chart. When they narrow, that is known as a volatility squeeze. If they spread out, that is a volatility spread.

- If the bands are narrow, that indicates that the prices over that period are falling within a smaller range (i.e. the closing prices for each period are relatively similar to each other).

- If the bands are wider, that indicates a greater spread in prices, that is individual prices differ from each other a lot more – put another way, there is more volatility.

What signals are there with Bollinger bands that a day trader can look for?

- If wick of a candlestick at the bottom hits the Bollinger band, that can be taken as a buy signal. The stock is oversold, so it's a good time to buy.

- When the candlestick touches or crosses the upper Bollinger band, then the stock is overbought. Time to sell.

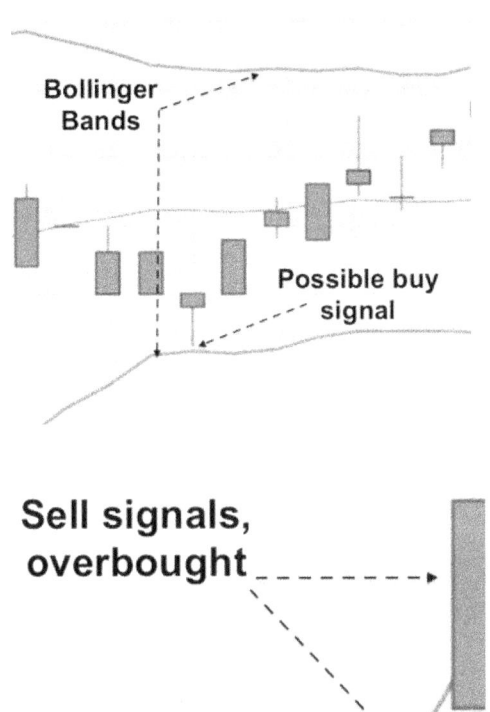

Of course, the vice versa applies, if a candle hits the top band, it may not be a sell signal, you may want to short or buy puts.

When the candlesticks are hitting the Bollinger bands, this may indicate a reversal. A hammer at the bottom of a reversal touching the bottom Bollinger band is a nice buy signal in many cases. Reversal candlesticks that touch a Bollinger band are a solid indicator that there is really a reversal coming.

In the opposite direction, if you are looking to short a stock or invest in puts, then you want to look for shooting stars that touch the upper Bollinger band. This can indicate a reversal or a coming downturn. If you are long on a stock and this condition arises, that indicates that it is a good time to sell.

When using Bollinger bands, you will want to look at the shape of the candlestick itself. This can strengthen or weaken your indicators. If you see a hammer at the bottom of the Bollinger bands, this can indicate a coming upturn in the stock so it's a good time to go long. On the other hand, if you see a shooting star touching the top Bollinger band, that may be an indicator that it is either a good time to sell or a good time to short or buy puts. Using Bollinger bands is not going to be a perfect indicator, but you can combine your observations about the shapes of the candlesticks and whether or not they are shooting stars or hammers together with the Bollinger bands to get a reasonable conjecture as to whether the stock is likely to move in one direction or in the opposite direction. In other words, looking at the candlesticks together with their relationship to the Bollinger bands will help you determine whether or not a given stock is primed to reverse.

Support and Resistance

We have touched on support and resistance earlier, here we will discuss the definitions in more detail. Support and resistance refer to lines on a pricing chart that act as barriers. That is, a support line will be found at the bottom of the chart that indicates a pricing level that serves as a minimum. Put another way, it is not expected that the price of the security in question will drop below the support. Looking toward increasing or higher prices, the resistance line is a top or maximum limit to expected changes in price. That is, it is not expected that the price of a security will go above the resistance line.

Support and resistance levels are primarily used to identify points at which the probabilities support a reversal, pause, or prevailing trend in the stock price. Since support is found at the bottom of a pricing chart, this means that the support represents a point where a downward trend can be expected to pause, and possibly reverse. On the other hand, the resistance is at the top of a stock pricing chart, hence it represents a point where an upward trend can be expected to pause, and possibly reverse and so turn into a downward trend. Of course, not all pauses result in reversals so you will have to look toward other signals such as the candlesticks and the Bollinger bands.

Trends in market activity are set by the basic economic principles of supply and demand. If the price of a security is dropping rapidly, the lower it drops the more demand for the stock is going to be generated. The support line represents the point at which demand is expected to overtake the selloff and possibly send the price of the stock upward again.

The resistance line works in converse fashion. As the price of a stock rises, at some point demand begins to slip. A sell-off begins which leads to declining prices.

A zone of support defines an entry point. That is, in simple language, this is a good point at which to buy the stock (go long or buy calls). This view, of course, may be in error. It's entirely possible that the stock can violate the price level and continue its decline until it hits new support, and a new entry point is defined.

Now let's consider a zone of resistance. This is where the stock price has been increasing. A zone of resistance defines a possible exit point. That is, it is expected (but not certain) that the stock is peaking out and this is a good time to get out. So if you are in a long position, in a zone of resistance you may want to sell. Once again, it is possible that the stock will violate the price level, and the zone of resistance may be an illusion as the stock begins to go up again until it reaches a new zone of resistance.

Traders act on the belief that a zone of support or resistance will not be broken. Of course, in many cases their bet is wrong. In that case, you can close and take a small loss. It's important to avoid letting emotions get the best of you in these situations. If you let emotion take over, you may hold onto your position too long hoping that somehow it can or will reverse course. Taking this approach can lead to larger losses. It's best to get out when you see the first signal that you've made an error.

So how do you spot a zone of resistance? Simply put, it's a price at which the stock approaches multiple times but can't seem to get past. You can define a zone of resistance over any time period you like, you could be talking about over an hour in the case of day trading or over the course of weeks or months for regular stock trading. If we take a hypothetical example, for XYZ stock it may see peaks at $98, $99.75, $99.50 and $99.85 over the course of a few hours. Then we may define the zone of resistance for that day at $100. A trader may decide to either short the stock, invest in puts, or if they are long, they may sell and close their position.

A zone of support works in the same way. There is a bottoming out price that the stock seems to keep approaching but doesn't cross and go lower. In that case, the trader may see this stock as a buying opportunity, it's a stock that is soon to rise in price. For the hypothetical XYZ stock, we could envision the zone of support being something like $90.

Trending is important when looking at support and resistance levels. It's not going to be very long that a stock is trapped in some zone where the level of support and resistance remains the same. It's going to be trending over time. With the changes in price, the support and resistance levels can change. For our hypothetical XYZ stock, if the company is healthy and growing, then we can imagine that it will eventually break the $100 barrier and climb up to a new level, say where the zone of resistance is $108, and the zone of support is $100. Depending on how volatile the stock is at a given moment, it could make this move quickly – within one single day.

It's useful to pay attention to moving averages when thinking about zones of support and resistance. When the moving average is below the actual price lines of the stock (that is the stock is trading at prices above the moving average), then that indicates a new zone of support. Conversely, when the stock is trading below the moving average, we have found a zone of resistance. Moving averages can also be used to look at the timing of when to enter and exit trades. If the price drops below the moving average, this indicates an exit point.

Risk

Formally defined, the risk is the difference between the entry price and the stop loss price. Suppose that stock XYZ is trading at $40. If you buy 100 shares of XYZ and then put in a stop-loss order of $35 a share, your risk is simply given by:

Risk = $40 - $35 = $5

Your position size is simply the number of shares that are bought in a given transaction.

Chapter 16 - Things You Should Not Do While Day Trading

Now that you know all of the things that you *should* do while you are day trading, you need to take a look at some of the things that you should be avoiding while you are day trading. Doing any of these things can hinder your ability to make money while you are trading and can cause major problems for you if you try to do them. They will not always destroy your day trading business but they have the potential to do so if you are not able to avoid them. Since it can be detrimental to your business, you should always try your best to stop these things before you even have a chance to start them.

Focus on One Strategy

Strategies are great and you absolutely need to have one if you are going to be trading but not having more than a single strategy can be detrimental in the event that you are not able to use that strategy. You should always make sure that you are working your hardest to build up many different strategies and that you are going to be able to do more with what you have. It can be hard to find more than one strategy that works for you and your business but if you are able to find one then you will be able to find more than one.

By allowing yourself to try different methods of trading, you will have more of an opportunity at getting the results that you want. This means that you need to make sure that you are learning as much as possible and that you are going to be able to try different things out. It can be complicated if you do not know what you are doing, but the easiest way to get started with methods of trading is to simply have a backup plan that you can use if your original trading plan does not go the way that you want. The backup plan with is your first alternative.

From there, you can learn even more methods of day trading. Fast selling, wait and watch approaches and trial and error are all a few different ways that you can make sure that you are getting the best experience possible when it comes to the various methods of trading.

Sit Back

Do not ever take a passive approach to trading. You should always be aggressive about your trades, make sure that you are doing everything that you can to be able to get the results that you want and always go after every single one of the trades that you are hoping for. It is a good idea to try different things to get there but don't sit back and wait for those to come to you. It will not only be detrimental to your efforts when it comes to trading but it can also be detrimental in that there are many different options that you can be missing out on.

If you are passive about the trading process, you will miss out on trades. There are no other traders who are successful and took a passive approach. It simply will not happen. Even when you are first getting started, it is important that you try to be as aggressive as possible so that you can get the results that you want. It makes more sense to push to get what you want than to sit and wait for it to just come to you. Trades don't work like that, and there is no magical way for you to get all of the stocks that you want – you have to put in the work and, sometimes, fight to be able to get them.

Do Too Much Effort

There is no reason that you should ever put more than a few hours on getting a stock. As a day trader, that is probably around 10% of your total day that you have available to trade. You don't want to waste it just chasing one thing and there are many different reasons that you may not want to continue chasing that one trade. One of the biggest reasons is that there is no guarantee that you are going to get a lot of money from it or that it will be profitable at all. There are too many other stocks that are available to you for you to waste all of your time on just one of them. It is important that you work toward getting different ones.

If you find that you have wasted too much time on one stock or one investment, you will not be able to get that time back, but you can try to make up for it by working twice as quickly at the other trading options. This means that you will sometimes need to double down your speed and not waste any time at all on the various trades. It also means that you can sometimes invest in trades that are going to be really bad for your overall profit. It is often just easier to chalk it up to a bad day and move on until the next day. If you can sell the stock that you wasted too much time on, that is beneficial and will allow you to, at least, recoup some of the money even if you can't get the time back.

Rely on Others

Nobody is going to hold your hand when it comes to trading. You need to make sure that you are working for yourself and that you are learning everything that you can on your own. While it is great to have the ability to learn from people who have come before you, they are not going to be the ones who show you what they can do. You need to learn the right way to do it all yourself and to get the most out of the experience of day trading. There are many different ways that you can teach yourself.

Don't rely on others. Rely only on yourself to make sure that you are going to be able to be the best at day trading. Reading this book is one of the easiest ways that you can start out your independent day trading career. Just reading this book is going to give you a great start and will allow you to see that you are truly going to be a great day trader. There are so many options from here that you can take your day trading career to the next level. It is important that you learn the right way to do it.

Stop Trading Out of Fear

If you don't take chances in trading, you will truly struggle to get to where you want to be. You need to take chances at not be afraid to trade something even if it seems like it is going to be a big risk. By allowing yourself the chance to see that good thing can come out of risky trades, you will be getting the upper hand when it comes to your day trading experience. There are many different options that you can enjoy but you will miss out on all of them if you are afraid to take a chance.

For this reason, it is important to weigh the benefits and the risks of trading. You need to figure out what is going to work for you and what is not going to work for you. If it seems like the trade that you are going to be making is going to be a huge risk, you may want to reconsider it. Always weigh the pros and the cons of a trade but also try to do some things that will scare you.

All in all, trading is a risk. You need to decide which smaller risks are things that you want to do and if they are worth it for your personal day trading career.

Chapter 17 - Trading and Commitment

Time is a tyrant, but not always! The first thing you have to concentrate on to put in place a good investment is the time you want to dedicate to the investment itself, or even to learn the new discipline with which you want to operate.

Our advice is to take all the time necessary to study the new techniques, to implement the new strategies, and to metabolize all the concepts well. Only after you have done this, we advise you to start trading in the stock market or trading with an online demo account.

Even if your investment objective is different from online trading, there's no problem. The important thing is to continue and persist in your own way to achieve the precise objective.

Have a Clear Goal

Another point on which we will focus is the investment objective. This point is very important for the trader and for his success also based on what is the psychology of an individual.

However, knowing how to do it is not a foregone conclusion. This presupposes a good capacity for analysis. In fact, in the investment, there is only the objective to be achieved; there is nothing but the possibility of victory and the possibility of losses and risks.

1)   Be the owner of your own money.

Being owners of their own money presupposes the possibility of being aware of recognizing one's own limits, having a precise objective and above all having the theoretical foundations to achieve it. In this sense, we must put ourselves in the advantageous condition of knowing which risks we can run. Recognizing them is really the starting point for a good investment. It would not make sense to start a new investment if you do not know the limits and do not know what the risks related to it are.

2)   Know yourself.

Once the first point has been made, and the objective is clear but also the risk related to the loss of one's own money, one has to do is start analyzing oneself. In this way, we can understand whether it is worthwhile trading with long-term strategies or short-term strategies, whether it is better to trade a certain capital rather than another, or better diversify investment objectives. It is better not to make fun of yourself if you do not want to lose your capital completely, you must recognize your limits, predict any reactions, and risk tolerance levels.

To better understand, let's take a practical example. Suppose we have two investment strategies. In both cases, the aim is to achieve 50% increase in initial capital. Based on what is in the first statistic, you can get a profit of 50% over a year, risking half the capital. According to the second strategy, on the other hand, we will obtain a profit of 50% over 2 years, but in a maximum period of 24 months, risking only 20% of the capital. At this point, a question arises: what kind of strategy to use?

In the first case, it is true that the goal is reached first, but it is also true that the percentages in case of loss are greater. If you come to check a negative period of time, even just three months, it is not easy not to consider it as a problem. Without making fun of it, nobody likes losing, and losing half of their capital can be a real blow to everyone.

But there is also the positive side; after the black period of three months, one could follow with half of the remaining capital and could concentrate on the remaining months to complete its strategy and make a profit. Once the negative moment has passed, the strategy begins to grind very good operations, and in the following 9 months, the account recovers not only the losses but closes positively with a further increase.

Now, this we have proposed to you is just one example. Not all traders close their accounts in a year. So, pay close attention. In the second case, however, the strategy can be used by all those who prefer to operate more safely and that we recommend because it limits the risk even if the waiting time is greater.

3) Objective = Earnings; Objective = Risk

Another important point to keep in mind and that must always be considered is what you want to earn, but above all, we are willing to risk to get that profit. Many times, it is more useful to rely on instinct and not on rationality, but this method does not always work. In this sense, we want to understand that it is much more prudent to evaluate the situation in which we find ourselves from time to time, to prefix the objectives we want to achieve at a given moment, and the possibility we have of reaching that goal. Therefore, knowing oneself before starting an investment is an excellent strategy to understand even the real goals and the real risks we can bear.

Chapter 18 - Exit Strategies

Many day traders are quite skilled and competent at entering positions. They have the ability, due to technical trading methods, experience, or a combination of the two, to time market entry precisely and with a high degree of accuracy. Their skills at exit methods, however, may well be sorely lacking. As a result, their inability to generate day trading profits proves even more frustrating than if their market entry methods were poor.

The purpose of this chapter is to discuss and illustrate a number of day trading exit techniques that will maximize your performance. You can also apply these profit maximizing strategies to other trading methods not covered here. Prior to giving you the details, I want to remind you that your ultimate results will always be a function of several variables as described below. No matter how promising a method or strategy may be, there are limitations on performance that are above and beyond what any ideal situation can anticipate. Your profits will be limited by:

• Follow-Through—Your ability to Follow-Through on a trading plan using discipline combined with an effective sense of market judgment.

• Limitations of pure day trading—Trading in periods of time longer than a day trade allows more flexibility on exit strategies and increases profit potential. Day trades inherently limit this.

• Ability to make subjective judgments—Day trading involves a certain amount of skill and judgment that cannot be totally mechanical if it is to be successful.

• Position size—Your success will be either enhanced by or limited by the size of your position (i.e., the number of shares or contracts you trade).

• Choice of markets—Your success will be enhanced or limited by the specific markets or stocks you trade in. Simply stated, some stocks and commodities are more conducive to day trading profits than are others. Some guidelines regarding selection criteria are provided at the end of this chapter.

The importance of position size

The day trader has several advantages over the position (longer-term) trader. First and foremost among these is that the result of the trade(s) will be known by the end of the day. Feedback is almost immediate, and it enhances learning. In addition to receiving prompt feedback on results, the pure day trader is, by definition, forced to take profits or losses by the end of the day, giving a daily performance report on total success or failure.

Many traders, out of their inability to accept losses (and a lack of discipline) will carry losing trades beyond their prescribed exit point and/or beyond the end of the trading day. One of the exit strategies I will discuss below suggests carrying part of a winning position beyond the end of the day. This is acceptable because the trade is profitable. Importantly, I do not, under any circumstances, advocate carrying a losing position to the next session.

The trade must be exited either at a stop loss, at a profit target, at a trailing stop, or at the end of the day. There is no ability to split the trade, that is, to allow profits to run while at the same time "taking some money off the table." In order to make profits consistently you will need to have large winning trades, unless you are highly accurate in your ability to repeatedly make small profits on small positions frequently. In my experience this is not easily or consistently achievable by most traders, unless they are on the trading floor where they are able to take advantage of very small price movements.

For most of us, the dream of being able to consistently reap small profits on small moves during the day is just that—a dream. I have seen many traders fail in their efforts to pursue this goal. Why? Because you may very well be able to achieve an amazing record of accuracy taking many small profits in a row—but a losing trade will eventually come, and it will often take all the previous profits or more.

As a result of this painful reality I urge you to consider trading in at least two units (i.e., lots of 100 shares of two futures contracts) so as to achieve more flexibility in an exit strategy that will allow you to carry winning positions. In so doing you will capture the largest profits, which will, in the end, make all the difference in your performance.

The "Pareto Principle" applies—at least 80 percent of your profits will be made on 20 percent of your trades. In order to make this market fact of life work for you, you will need to let part of your positions ride for maximum profits. There are several ways to do this. Here are a few general approaches.

Exit strategies for single unit trading

If you're limited by circumstances or by choice to trade in single units—a single futures contract or 100-share unit of stock—your choices and profit potential may be limited. However, you can still succeed if you follow one or more of the strategies below. You will, though, be limited in how much profit you can take. Given this limitation you have several choices.

1. Stick to trading methodology. Take profits at a profit target that is generated by your trading methodology. Do not take profits based on "gut feel" or intuition. Use a specific method to arrive at your target, and use it consistently. The good news in taking profits at a profit target is that you will have banked the money. The bad news is that you will lose your ability to participate in a larger move. I have already stated why this is not preferable unless you can achieve and maintain very high accuracy while limiting losses to relatively small amounts.

2. Look for a break-even target. Determine a profit target that, if and when met, will be your cue to place a stop loss at break even. Break even is defined as your entry price. This will allow you to remove most of the risk from your trade while also allowing you to hold the position. If you are not stopped out, then you can exit at the end of the session. The good news is that you will have given yourself more opportunity to take the bigger profit. The bad news is that you may be stopped out repeatedly at break even. But is that really bad news? Think about it!

3. Look for a second profit target. You can implement strategy number two as noted above and use a trailing stop procedure once a second profit target has been achieved. In other words, once the first profit target is achieved, enter the stop loss to keep the break-even intact and watch for the realization of a second profit target. If you use a second profit target, it should also be based on a consistent logic and/or method. This will avoid the placement of profit targets willy-nilly.

I recommend either strategy two or three as the preferred approach for one position (i.e., 100 shares of stock or one futures contract).

Exit strategies for two-unit trading

Trading in two units gives you considerably more flexibility and will return larger profits in the long run. Here are your choices:

1. Half-position closeout. Take profits on one half of your position at a profit target that is generated by your trading methodology. Do not take profits based on "gut feel" or intuition. Use a specific method to arrive at your target and use it consistently. The good news in taking profits at a profit target is that you will have banked the money. The better news is that you will still have part of your position, which you can carry for a larger profit.

2. Place a stop loss on the remainder of the position. The profit target, if and when met, will be your cue to place a stop loss at break even on the remainder of the position. Break even is defined as your entry price. This will allow you to remove most of the risk from your trade while allowing you to hold the second position. If you are not stopped out, then you can exit at the end of the session. The good news is that you will have given yourself more opportunity to take the bigger profit. The bad news is that

you may be stopped out repeatedly at break even on this second position.

3. Setup a second profit target on the second position. You can implement strategy number two as noted above and use a trailing stop procedure once on the second position. You can also use a second profit target if you wish. If you use a second profit target please be sure that it is based on a consistent logic and/or method. The old rules still apply. Regardless of what you do, the position is closed out by the end of the session.

I recommend either strategy two or three as the preferred approach for two positions (i.e., 200 shares of stock or two futures contracts).

The preferred approach

From experience, I prefer trading in units of three positions. Here's how it works:

1. Take profits on first third. Take profits on one third of your position at a profit target that is generated by your trading methodology. Again, do not take profits based on "gut feel" or intuition. Use a specific method to arrive at your target and use it consistently. Then, hold one third of

the remaining position with a break even stop. Hold one third of the position with a trailing stop that can be implemented immediately or when a second target is hit. The good news in taking profits at a profit target is that you will have banked part of the profit. The better news is that you will still have two-thirds of your position, which you can carry for a larger profit.

2. Use second profit target. You can implement strategy number one as noted above and use a break-even-based trailing stop procedure once on the second position. You can also use a second profit target if you wish. If you use a second profit target, please be sure that it is based on a consistent logic and/or method. Regardless of what you do, the second part of your position is closed out by the end of the session.

3. Use third profit target. You can exit another third of your position by the end of the session or you can exit the balance of the position by the end of the session. You can keep the profit target up and implement additional trailing stops. You can also implement a variety of trailing stop and/or profit target possibilities. As you can see, there is considerable flexibility. The key to the entire strategy is to

get out of the danger zone with an initial break even stop loss and lock in at least some profit (i.e., initial stop loss) as soon as a profit target is hit, then build from there. I cannot emphasize this aspect strongly enough.

4. Beyond day's end. For those who seek adventure, one third of the position can be carried beyond the end of the session, but it should be noted that in so doing you will no longer be in a day trade, and you will no longer qualify for day trade margin on that position. Furthermore, you will risk exposure of an opening price that may turn your profits into a loss.

I recommend either strategy two, three, or four as the preferred approach for three positions (i.e., 300 shares of stock or three futures contracts).

The suggestions noted above are applicable to virtually any of the methods I have discussed in this book. Next, let's take a look at some technical methods for trailing stops.

Trailing stop strategies

By "trailing stop" I mean the use of a buy stop or a sell stop that is designed to capture or lock in a percentage of the open profit on a position. By definition, a trailing stop (TS) is a stop that is changed every time the open profit in a trade reaches a new peak. It follows a few increments behind the price movement, up or down. Trailing stops on a profitable long position, for example, are always moving higher as the underlying market is moving in your favor. A trailing stop on a long position is never lowered. The opposite holds true for a trailing stop on a short position, which is never raised.

Chapter 19 - The Secrets of Successful Day Traders

You have gone through all the basics of day trading and I hope you absorbed all the quality information I provided to you.

They are equally important as every other information in this eBook because you need to avoid some of the mistakes I am going to point out as well as concentrate on some good things and facts I am going to mention in the next couple of paragraphs.

I would like this chapter to be about pointing you out the mistakes you can make in day trading that could keep you away from success and profit.

I believe I found seven big mistakes any day trader can make. Do you know what does that actually mean? Your chances to fail are much bigger than to succeed.

1. Mistake #1: Over-analyzing

The problem people usually make in day trading is that they over-analyze the market to find a trend. This approach is often very wrong and there is a misconception among people that says *"more complicated formula and algorithm you have, the better are the odds for making profit."*

That is simply not true. Yes, it is good to have a formula and algorithm you follow but you cannot forget one of the most important rules in day trading. *You buy when the market is going up and sell when the market is going down.*

2. Mistake #2: Not taking your profits

Do you know why only 1 out of 10 people reach success in day trading? It is because 9 out of 10 people are greedy. It is not a get-rich-quick scheme and success is possible only if you are patient.

3. Mistake #3: Not limiting losses

That is not strange, not even to most successful day traders. They lose money, too. A lot! But they are successful because they know how to limit their losses. I will repeat it again. It is of extreme importance to know when to exit a certain trade to save money. It is always better to lose $300 than $3000 because you stayed to long.

4. Mistake #4: Sticking with the wrong market

I am sure that you are going to reach success with certain type of market. The question is whether you will tie yourself to the same market forever. You need to follow the market! YOU NEED TO BE THE MARKET!

Another important fact is that you need to be in the market that is moving because, as I repeatedly say, buy when the market goes up and sell when it goes down. From that, we can conclude that you need to be okay with changes and adapting on new markets constantly. Go where the money is, and money is never in the steady market.

5. Mistake #5: Not developing a trading strategy

If you think you can succeed in today's world, in any profession, without a plan and a strategy, you are terribly wrong. No one can do that.

6. Not controlling yourself

When people describe me, they usually say that I am an incredibly calm person. This is because I learned how to control my emotions and my thoughts because if you do not control thoughts, they will control you.

Calmness should be the main characteristic of every successful trader. If you do not how to control your greediness, your fear or your panic, you will never succeed.

7. Overtrading

Finally, yet importantly, learn when it is enough. I think I talked about this on every seminar I had about day trading. Overtrading is common problem of every day trader.

When you reach your weekly goals, just stop! There is no reason to keep trading if you already made the profit you want.

People usually make these seven mistakes. I know you need to avoid them if you want profit.

Now I am going to list some of the characteristics of successful day traders. Pay attention if you want to develop some serious skills:

They do not blame other people because of their losses and failures. They think that is normal and there is no reason to blame your broker or any other person because you lost money on certain trade.

They have a system. In the system, they developed every possible situation that can happen.

They do not stay in the losing trade and they do not hurry and rush into trades. They are precise, they take their time and they are well aware of each step they make. That is why they are successful.

They learned how to adapt. Maybe I didn't stress out how this is important in day trading because market constantly changes and if you want to keep having profits, you need to go with the change.

Conclusion

Thanks for downloading this book. I know I have said this before but I have to emphasize this point again. Eventually when you have navigated yourself a little in the stock market, you will have to settle down on something that suits your personality. Some people have more appetite for risk and may have better results with swing trading while some people do much better with momentum day trading. Your goal is to find your niche as soon as possible and stick with it. You either find your niche by paper trading and testing your results, or testing the stock market with a small amount of real money. For many new traders, it is often very tempting to just dive straight into the market with all your money. My advice is to take everything slowly and focus on learning and absorbing quality information at first. You have to remember that even the most successful traders are still students of the market.

There is a fine line between passion and obsession. If you find yourself throwing more and more savings into your brokerage account without knowing WHY, you are hooked to this game and you better GET OUT. If you are a great trader, you will never be obsessed with trading because you control your own emotions. Never EVER let your guard down to the emotional side of you during trading, because a gentle misstep can and will cause an avalanche.

Many great traders I know are truly passionate about trading, they are very focused on their charts and rarely make mistakes in their trades. But they also rarely step away from the trading desk and all they see are charts and numbers. They eat and sleep thinking about stock charts. Life is not all about trading, whenever I made a good profit for the day, I will step away from the trading desk and hang out with some friends or family. You don't have to be greedy because trading opportunities will come every single day. Place your loved ones on the top of your priority list because they will be the ones to support you when you fall.